A World of Men

The MIT Press

Cambridge, Massachusetts, and
London, England

A World of Men
The Private Sources
of American Foreign
Policy

Lloyd S. Etheredge

This book was set in IBM Composer Univers by To the
Lighthouse Press, printed and bound by Halliday
Lithograph Corporation in the United States of
America.

Library of Congress Cataloging in Publication Data

Etheredge, Lloyd S.
  A world of men.

  Bibliography: p.
  Includes index.
  1. United States—Foreign relations administration—Research.   2. United States—Diplomatic and
consular service.   I. Title.
JX1706.E83   327.73   78—9122
ISBN 0-262-05019-6

For my parents and
brother

Contents

Acknowledgments

I am grateful to a large number of people and institutions for financial support, advice, and constructive criticism over the seven years that have elapsed since the two studies that make up this book were first envisioned.

The National Institute of Mental Health, through its funding of the Psychological Study of Politics program at Yale University, was an important catalyst for this research. The fellowship support provided me as part of this program is gratefully acknowledged, though, since my conclusions may be seen as critical of presidents and the US State Department, it is important to emphasize that NIMH played no specific role in, and bears no responsibility for, my research or my conclusions.

An early teacher, Robert W. Tufts of Oberlin, helped to demythologize American foreign policy and interested me in its personal sources. Beginning as a doctoral thesis at Yale, these studies have been strengthened by the criticism and advice of Paul Berman, Robert E. Lane, John McConahay, and H. Bradford Westerfield. James David Barber advised on the historical study. Harold D. Lasswell was a continuing source of inspiration, interest, and professional support that was both generous and gracious.

The Department of Political Science and the Office of Advanced Political Studies at Yale provided financial support for the questionnaire study and for preliminary data analysis. The Research Board and Department of Political Studies at the University of Manitoba (Canada) provided additional computer and secretarial support. Since 1975 I have been grateful to the Department of Political Science at M.I.T. for secretarial and other support for the successive versions of the manuscript.

Lynn Etheredge, Barbara Torrey, David Biltchik, John Hurley, Don Ellson, and Lt. Colonel James Nelson assisted me in bringing an invitation to participate in the questionnaire study to the attention of people at the State Department, the National War College, and the Office of Management and Budget.

I have been aided in various ways by many other people too numerous to mention, but I want especially to acknowledge appreciation to Charles Heck and the late Conrad Morrow who served as coders for the historical study and to the late Jeff Pressman. Valuable comments on individual chapters or versions of the entire manuscript have been provided by Chris Achen, Hayward Alker, Lance Bennett, Jere Bruner, Lynn Etheredge,

Alexander George, Fred Greenstein, Ole Holsti, Irving Lefberg, Ken Mc-Vicar, and David Rothberg.

Colleagues and graduate students at M.I.T. have provided a congenial environment in which to complete this manuscript—cordial, tough-minded and candid, diverse.

I want to express special appreciation to the men and women at the State Department, National War College, and Office of Management and Budget for their participation, which made possible this analysis of their foreign policy thinking.

Finally, I want to thank the secretaries who worked on successive versions of the manuscript: Jackie Baizley, Evelyn Fieldhouse, Gail Lopata, Marion Marden, Donna McVicar, Rose Schertow, Julie Velasquez, and Linda Woolford.

An earlier version of chapter 6 appeared in the *American Political Science Review* and that chapter appears here by kind permission of the American Political Science Association.

Tables

Introduction

This book presents conclusions from two investigations of the psychological sources of American foreign policy thinking, and, in particular, of American wars. The first investigation is a detailed study of the minds of a random sample (N = 126) of career foreign service officers at the State Department, a study supplemented by comparison data from military officers and from domestic policy specialists. It is the first broad study, with career specialists, of ten theories of how emotional predispositions might shape elite foreign policy thinking.

The second study analyzes actual top level decisions, 62 major cases of decision disagreements (49 of them involving the use of force) among American presidents, secretaries of state, and selected advisers from 1898 to 1968. This historical study, the first systematic examination of the foreign policy consequences of American presidents' personalities, confirms substantial personality effects on our foreign policy—and specifically documents such effects on the decision to use military force.

The message of these two studies is the conclusion, based on hard data, that American wars and major errors in foreign policy decisions are not behind us but result partly from psychological processes which maintain a *continuing* place in international relations. War (especially against smaller countries) and error are more likely as in part a predictable consequence of American elite composition and the psychology of American foreign policy decision making.

Several specific conclusions for which evidence will be presented in the following chapters include:

• Frequently, although not always, major American diplomatic and military decisions (including war) are crucially determined by personal forces arising from within the decision maker. These forces affect judgment systematically and are not selectively attuned to the constraints of reality.

• Major beliefs about the Soviet Union arise partly from the imagination of the decision maker himself and may often tell more about the decision maker than about the Russians.

• The conviction of decision makers that they make rational choices based exclusively on realistic assessments of the world seems to be based partly on confidence that is an unrecognized effect of the use of intuition.

• While the personality makeup of males who strive for, and are selected for, high American office often makes them ambivalent about the use of force, the personality makeup of presidents and foreign policy elites contains those ingredients—and in significant measure—that make war more likely.

• It is likely that these results would hold for other world leaders and not only for American presidents and foreign policy elites.

My impression is that people who hold idealized images of presidents and other high officials can find these conclusions disillusioning and that disillusionment leaves them feeling vulnerable and scared. As well, foreigners, who are among the potential victims of these processes, also have found them unsettling. I want to caution against concluding that "you can't trust the power elites," because sometimes these elites do make competent and wise decisions. But this book does suggest it would be realistic to be skeptical of the men—both in America and elsewhere—who hold power and make decisions.

The conclusions in the foregoing list—involving, as they do, a revised image of the history of America's foreign policy since 1898, a revised image of the (apparently substantial) importance of personality in foreign policy formulation, and an implicit critique of men in public life who substitute self-confidence for hard evidence—may be controversial. Or, on the other hand, perhaps they are obvious. Earlier reactions to my public discussion of these data have ranged widely. One diplomatic historian thought my conclusions about the major effects of presidential personality and American elite psychology were "obvious," and he was bemused by social scientists "hacking their way through open doors." A former high State Department official quickly dismissed the whole enterprise on the grounds the decisions he participated in were "too complex" to be explained by someone who was not there. One student angrily asserted that President Johnson "would never have allowed his personality to intrude" on his major decisions because these decisions were too serious and our national leaders "have too much integrity to send American soldiers to die because of personal motives." Indeed, the issue of whether these conclusions are obvious or controversial seems itself to be controversial.

My own view, discussed in chapter 5, is that—regardless of whether these conclusions have been obvious all along to some outside observers—the people *involved* in foreign policy have not been explicitly aware of the personal forces shaping their own thoughts and perceptions. To be sure, each man can readily believe that people who differ from himself are irrationally influenced, but he does not see that his own views and his own confidence and sense of rational superiority are in part the result of the same subjective mechanisms operating in other people whose ideas he considers suspect.

A final word about my title, *A World of Men*. It reflects three considerations. First, the world of power politics (and almost everyone I have studied) is male. Second, the effects of the heroic ambition, competitiveness, dominance, and power motivation of a substantial number of these men seem specifically to implicate what is known in psychology as a "male narcissism syndrome": to this extent the fact that virtually all American and world political leaders have been male probably increases the likelihood of war. Third, the title is intended to resonate with "men," used in a generic sense, in the quotation at the beginning of chapter 7: "A world of science and great machines is still a world of men." Technology, for all its glamour, has the unfortunate potential of multiplying any malfunction of the mind of a political leader by millions of times. The ancient anger of Zeus would unleash only a few lightning bolts, but the unrealistic ambitions or erroneous fears of a modern American or Soviet leader can destroy, with nuclear explosions, most of the life in the Northern Hemisphere. For reasons I do not understand, the amount of money and effort devoted to the study of how political leaders can learn to be more competent at their jobs is miniscule. By my title and the use of the quotation I mean to imply that the world has a need to develop more thoughtful and wise leaders; that is more pressing than the need to develop impressive and expensive weapons.

A World of Men

1 The Problem of Mistakes in Foreign Policy

When a hungry cat concentrates his attention on a mousehole, there usually is a mouse in it; but when the government of some great country has concentrated its attention and efforts on some particular foreign-policy objective, the outcome remarkably often has been unrewarding. ... During the half century from 1914 to 1964, the decisions of major powers to go to war or to expand a war, and their judgments of the relevant intentions and capabilities of other nations, seem to have involved major errors of fact, perhaps in more than 50% of all cases.

Karl W. Deutsch
The Analysis of International Relations

Soon after he was elected president, John F. Kennedy was briefed about a proposed American-supported invasion of Cuba. In the months that followed the president and his advisers considered the recommendation, altered details, and, finally, the president ordered the invasion by a force of Cuban refugee guerillas at the Bay of Pigs.

Compared with the crisis conditions under which world leaders often must decide whether or not to use force, Kennedy and his advisers enjoyed both exceptional freedom from pressure and a great deal of time for careful thought and analysis. There was no surprise, no crisis atmosphere, no imminent threat of nuclear war, no necessity for rapid judgment.[1] Moreover the president's advisers were, in David Halberstam's phrase, among "the best and the brightest" in America's foreign policy establishment.[2] If one were to choose circumstances in which the decision to use force in world politics would be the result of and reflect analytic brilliance and realism of the highest order, it would have been this group and this situation that would have been chosen.

But the consequence of President Kennedy's decision was dramatic and total failure. The dream of success that was so attractive to the president and his advisers shattered before reality, and victory that seemed so plausible was a decisive defeat.[3]

What produced such a wrong decision in this case? An answer to this question is probably important to a broader understanding of international politics: as Karl Deutsch notes in the quotation at the beginning of this chapter, serious mistakes by top decision makers are actually common in international politics. In fact, between 1914 and 1968 the initiators of violence lost 60% of their wars, evidence of pervasive miscalculation and overconfidence if we assume a country should only begin a military action when it will win.[4] To take several major examples: the instigators of World War I lost. There is no evidence that either Hitler or Japanese leaders consciously wanted a self-defeating nightmare from World War II. Kennedy did not want to lose at the Bay of Pigs. Soviet Premier Khrushchev did not want nuclear confrontation and a humiliating face-down in the Cuban missile crisis. President Johnson did not want ultimate defeat when he escalated the Vietnam War. The track record of world leaders has been remarkably poor. It will be a safer world if we can diagnose the sources of these errors and prevent them in the future.

Many reasons have been advanced to explain the faulty Bay of Pigs decision. The most thoughtful of these analyses argue there were defects in the decision-making processes employed in the Kennedy administration.[5] But, without ruling out the importance of good decision-making processes, my attention has been drawn to another area, the personality of the key decision makers. Social scientists interested in political psychology have begun to identify systematic linkages between the personality characteristics and the official actions of presidents, premiers, judges, lawmakers, and other political notables.[6] Of course, decision makers believe they are rational, realistic men, and decisions are justified by reference to facts, to broad principles and ideals, to the public interest. But the observation that most major foreign policy decisions provoke disagreement suggests that such decisions may have personal and private origins which are masked by the rationales ultimately offered for public consumption.

One could hold that imperfect decision-making processes were central to President Kennedy's unrealistic Bay of Pigs decision if Kennedy had been the captive of a group of unanimous advisers. But President Kennedy did not simply rubber-stamp the unanimous recommendations of others: a well-informed journalist, recently returned from Cuba, told the president privately that the hoped-for mass uprising was doubtful; adviser Arthur Schlesinger, Jr., opposed the plan in a long memorandum to the president; Senator J. William Fulbright, then chairman of the Senate Foreign Relations Committee, spoke strongly in opposition.[7] Kennedy made his decision in the face of disagreement and ambiguity. Kennedy *did* hear doubts; he chose to discount them. What led Kennedy to override such ultimately realistic doubts and order this plan?

Certain aspects of President Kennedy's personality might explain his decision to launch a guerilla invasion. Throughout his life he evidenced a pattern of being attracted to stories of men who, starting from subordinate positions and with odds and powerful forces arrayed against them, finally emerged heroically triumphant. He had written *Profiles in Courage,* a study of such men. He particularly enjoyed Ian Fleming's novels about a secret agent, James Bond, who triumphed miraculously against the awesome forces of SMERSH. He was fascinated by guerilla warfare, he devoted personal attention to the Army's training program for its Special Forces, and he insisted—against Army resistance—that the Special Forces have a distinctive uniform and be an elite corps.[8] Such themes resonated with similar patterns of heroic striving in Kennedy's own life: his courageous survival when his boat, PT-109, was destroyed during World War II; his survival after a near-fatal back operation; his long-standing competition with—and eventual replacement of—his older brother Joseph, whom Kennedy's father had wished to be president; his remarkable grass-roots political organization and success in winning the presidential nomination from the established regulars of the Democratic party; his winning of the presidency at a comparatively young age.

President Kennedy was a man who imagined a world full of challenges, challenges which he also imagined could be overcome by men (like himself) embodied with drive, courage, and vision. He selected many such men as his advisers. The rhetoric, dreams, and activity of the New Frontier show that these personal tendencies probably were generalized onto domestic political issues (often with beneficial results) and stated rhetorically as being in the public interest. Such generalization also occurred in nonmilitary areas of foreign policy—for example in the rhetoric and ambitions of the Peace Corps and Alliance for Progress which Kennedy initiated. In military matters the attraction of guerilla and counterguerilla activities went far beyond details of uniforms and instruction in the Army. At Kennedy's direction much attention was paid to these issues in his administration as a whole, and numerous

officials from the State and Defense departments were sent through sem-
inars to update their thinking.[9] And President Kennedy favored, in situations in which other men disagreed, both the guerilla invasion of Cuba and
the introduction of American Special Forces advisers to bolster the South
Vietnamese government.

Thus a case can be made that President Kennedy's personality was the
crucial ingredient in producing the Bay of Pigs decision. We would predict,
on the basis of Kennedy's personality and pattern of behavior in other
areas, that he would be more predisposed than men with different traits to
perceive Fidel Castro and communism in Latin America as a challenge,
that he would be more predisposed to favor heroic action to meet such a
challenge, that he would be more predisposed to believe the Cuban challenge would be overcome successfully by brave and committed men in a
guerilla invasion force.

But this explanation, a working hypothesis, might be hasty and mis-
leading. It is an explanation constructed after the fact. There is not yet
reliable and broadly based evidence that men in responsible positions of
national leadership allow their personalities to intrude in a decisive way
when the well-being of their nations and the lives of many on both sides
are at stake.

This book deals with such issues in a more general framework, assessing
the evidence from a range of situations with multiple indicators to determine whether there exists a general pattern of personality intrusion in
determining America's use of military force. Following a review of relevant
theory in chapter 2, a detailed study of the psychology of a random sample of 126 career foreign service officers at the State Department (and
comparison groups of military officers and domestic policy professionals)
in chapters 3-5 establishes evidence for such a pattern of personality influence on both policy attitudes and images of reality among professional
mid-elites, an intrusion which is a consequence of the intuitive methods
these men use to understand an ambiguous, uncertain world and which
operates to produce a self-deceptive confidence that choices are rational.
In chapter 6 a historical comparison of presidents and secretaries of state
between 1898 and 1968 finds convergent evidence, using different
methods, that similar personality effects have tilted the balance of a decision for or against the use of force in actual decisions: the Bay of Pigs

decision is revealed to be a member of a class of decisions that includes (among others) Woodrow Wilson's punitive policies toward Mexico, the Dulles militarization of the containment doctrine during the 1950s, and Lyndon Johnson's escalation of the Vietnam War.

The enterprise that follows should be clear in two respects: first, the logic of the exercise is to assess the effects of personality differences *while holding situations constant.* This book is not designed to propose a total theory of international behavior, let alone argue the unwarranted conclusion that American foreign policy is solely the direct expression of the depth psychology of presidents. Kennedy may have invaded Cuba and Johnson the Dominican Republic in part because of their personal predispositions, but these decisions did not happen in the reverse order—Kennedy chose Cuba and not the Dominican Republic partly because of the *situation* in Cuba at the time. Any comprehensive theory of international relations would also have to be a theory of contexts, and not only (as in this study) a theory of decision making within these contexts.

Second, it is important to understand how the statement that personality-based decision making is risky is itself warranted by the studies reported here. This conclusion can, I think, be drawn fairly even without reaching prior agreement on the best policy or the most appropriate image of reality in each case. Take the example of a study which finds that some automobile drivers tend systematically to steer into a curve or to drive straight ahead (*and* to believe their decision reflects a realistic assessment of road conditions) *because of something arising from within themselves rather than only from the objective shape of the road ahead.* We would, I think, agree that these are dangerous drivers, even if they are well intentioned. It is by a like recognition that I conclude that existing decision-making methods are risky. Unfortunately (as I will discuss in chapter 7), it is unlikely that completely safe alternatives are available.

It should also be clear that, although this work highlights personality intrusions that produce the use of force, the data actually shown that doves, hawks, and those in between are equally likely to base policies on self-expression, and their images of reality on intuitions shaped by personal psychodynamics. Dovish humanism does not emerge with a superior claim to be more objectively based among these men.

2 The Context and Processes of Personality Influence

If you ask a man why he believes what he does, why he is a liberal or conservative or isolationist or whatever, and if he does not think you impertinent, he is likely to tell you about the world and not about himself. . . . In the space of a minute or two he will have given you a brief model of the world as he understands it, something of the way he sees, feels, and thinks; but you will go away, perhaps rather sooner than you had planned, with information relevant to only one interpretation of the question.

Suppose you had said, "Yes, but why are *you* a conservative?" tilting the question around so that it faces him rather than the world . . .

Robert E. Lane
Political Thinking and Consciousness

Wars, like chemical explosions, may result from varied combinations of many different elements. There have been aggressive wars for territorial expansion or material advantage. There have been wars of liberation. There have been preventive or defensive wars. There have been civil wars. There have been religious crusades. There have been tribes or societies that seem to have gone to war simply for glory or because they liked to fight.[1]

The concern in this book is not to develop a general theory of all these wars or even of one war. Rather it is the limited problem of tracing the effect of certain aspects of the personality of the decision maker upon the decision to go to war. One war might be explained by the factors $A + B + C + D + X$, another by the factors $C + D + K + Q + X$. It is how an X-factor, the personality of the decision maker, operates within different situations that will be the focus here.

The major part of this chapter is devoted to examining different theories of how elements of a decision maker's personality might influence his judgments and images of reality.

Theorists have engaged in continuing debate over the problems of whether, and if so, how, the personal qualities of a top level decision maker affect his perceptions and decisions.[2] A traditional view skeptical of the influence of personal traits grows from the assumption that both international politics and government decision making are so highly organized that, for every major decision, any decision maker will face a set of objective forces which impel his decision and that by selection, professional training, and organizational norms, elite decision makers are "standard-

ized" to respond to these objective forces in predictable ways regardless of
personal preference.

This skeptical position has much to recommend it. In fact there *are*
many views held in common among the men I studied; as chapter 3 will
show, a substantial majority agree that the Soviet Union is slightly or
moderately menacing to American interests but England is seen as friendly.
A substantial majority would use American force to prevent a Soviet naval
buildup in the Caribbean, while a substantial majority stated that they
would have opposed American military intervention in Indonesia in the
1960s. There are, as the skeptical position suggests, external factors which
produce very substantial shifts to different perceptions and to different
policy recommendations even when the distribution of personality traits
is held constant.

Still, it is too much to say that factors external to the decision maker
solely determine his images of reality and whether he decides to use force.
Reading the daily newspaper reveals significant elite disagreements over
foreign policy. And as will be shown in chapters 4 and 5, there are consequential personality-based disagreements among these men in their tendencies to feel either threatened or relaxed about the Soviet Union's
intentions and in their tendencies to use or oppose force. The historical
study of presidents and secretaries of state between 1898 and 1968 in
chapter 6 will present evidence that the personality of the president has in
a substantial number of cases since 1898 tipped the balance decisively for
or against the use of force, especially in situations involving American
military intervention in small countries. While the X-factors of personal
predisposition can be overridden by powerful external forces, often there
is sufficient ambiguity so that the contribution of these X-factors of
personality is consequential for crystallizing a specific image of reality
and a specific course of action.

The Decision Maker and His Decision

Psychologists and political scientists have devoted considerable effort
to the problem of clarifying personal sources of foreign policy deci-

sions.[3] One useful set of categories is a schema which thinks of judgments as formed in relation to four different aspects of the individual: (1) his *values,* (2) his *cognitive capabilities and processes,* (3) his *emotional dynamics and predispositions,* and (4) the *interaction of himself with his surroundings*—i.e., with the social consensus and structure of the group to which he belongs and others whose opinions are important to him.[4]

Some work, although far too little, has been devoted to the problem of values, especially to *unrealizable values* as a source of policies which are unproductive or disastrous. Fitzgerald, for example, maintains that America's recent efforts to nurture Vietnam's emergence as a Western-style democracy could never have succeeded.[5]

The greatest density of research has centered upon analyzing and improving cognitive processes. One approach has been to consider the problems of thinking and learning of foreign policy decision makers as an extension of those cognitive processes found to be generally true of the mind.[6] Another approach, being actively pursued by Alexander George and Ole Holsti, is to study individual differences in thinking about the world—a man's assumptions, his categories, his "operational code," the lessons he has learned from his past experiences.[7]

The third aspect of the individual, his emotional dynamics and predispositions, has also been investigated through two approaches, the first dealing with emotional dynamics common across individuals (stress responses, especially during crisis; and aggression, especially that resulting from frustration).[8] The second approach, represented specifically in the studies undertaken here, looks at individual differences in personality traits and the impact of these differences in producing different policies and perceptions.[9]

The fourth aspect that can be made the subject of research is how attitudes and policies are shaped by contexts of interpersonal and organizational relationships. Janis's concept of the "groupthink" syndrome has been a major contribution to an understanding of these processes;[10] Argyris's study of the ways interpersonal and organizational norms in the State Department inhibit performance of its responsibilities is another.[11] The literature on "bureaucratic politics," dealing in part with how a person's

job affects his viewpoint, also bears on this aspect of an attitude formation.[12]

This brief sketch locates the present work within the context of work
by others. This book is primarily an investigation of the effect of individual differences in the third (emotional dynamics) of the four categories
upon foreign policy decisions.

Theories of The Influence of Personality on Policy and on Perception

The State Department study to be discussed in chapters 3-5 is based upon
five traditional theories about personality effects on policy ((a1) interpersonal generalization, (a2) displacement of subjective fantasy goals,
(a3) inverse interpersonal generalization, (a4) defects in mental health
that would produce deviations from cooperative internationalism, and
(a5) the interaction of personality with organizational setting) and upon
five theories about the effects of personality on perception ((b1) self-
based inference, (b2) attribution (i.e., projection) of subjective fantasy
goals, (b3) inverse self-based inference, (b4) defects in mental health
that would produce systematic effects on reality-testing, and (b5) the
interaction of personality with organizational setting). The reason for
testing these theories was not to determine whether they were true or
false in a total sense—there is already evidence that each explains something about some members of the general public. Rather the purpose of
testing was to determine their *applicability* to these specific men in the
area of their foreign policy thinking.[13]

Let me briefly review each of the approaches incorporated into the
study.

Personality Effects on Policy
Interpersonal Generalization (a1)

Interpersonal generalization theory proposes that decision makers relate to
other nations in ways that are straightforward extensions of their manner
of relating to people in their daily lives. A classic study in this tradition was
conducted by Bjorn Christiansen with 167 cadets and applicants at the

Military and Naval Academies in Oslo.[14] Each man was presented with
written descriptions of 40 potential everyday conflicts and asked how he
would likely react and with written descriptions of 40 potential international conflicts and asked how he wished Norway to react. Christiansen
found, for example, that in an everyday situation where a friend absent-
mindedly burned a large hole on the subject's table with a lighted ciga-
rette, those who would angrily reproach him and tell him to watch what
he is doing were more likely, if a Russian radio station jammed Norwegian
foreign broadcasts, to be blaming and punitive in this international situation as well, to want Norway to protest and retaliate by jamming Russian
foreign broadcasts. Correlations between six everyday and six international response tendencies were statistically significant at the $< .01$ level,
averaged about $r = .40$, and provided striking evidence that men who
blame and threaten others in everyday conflicts also favored blaming and
threatening other nations in international conflicts.[15] Christiansen's study
did not show, however, whether or not such generalization extended to
the predisposition to advocate a war (war was not a plausible option for
Norway at the time). However, more recent research in this tradition with
Americans shows that such a generalization does occur (at least in samples
of the general public) to product magnification of interpersonal responses.
For example, Americans who believe children need strict discipline from
their parents are more inclined to advocate use of nuclear weapons in international conflicts. In the terms of William Eckhardt's review and factor
analysis, a general predisposition to use self-assertive "compulsion" of
others is generalized and magnified into advocacy of punitive responses in
American foreign policy.[16]

Displacement of Subjective Fantasy Goals (a2)

My guess, which I tested as a theory, was that men differ in how they
would like ideally to feel about themselves, and that differences in such
fantasies for desired feeling-states were displaced in the selection of policies with the desired connotation. Specifically, I suspected a man sought
(possibly to gain vicarious satisfaction) for his nation to adopt those policies which symbolized his ideal self. An ambitious man who wished to feel
active, powerful, and influential would advocate more militaristic, activist
policies for his nation; a man whose wishes were for a relatively pastoral

and tranquil state of mind would advocate nonmilitary, low key policies.[17]

Inverse Interpersonal Generalization (a3)

A third theoretical tradition derives from early work in anthropology: Sumner's *Folkways,* published in 1906, proposed a causal relationship between ingroup solidarity and hostility toward outgroups.[18] Such "ethnocentrism" predicts, at least in one formulation, the exact opposite of interpersonal generalization. Interpersonal generalization theory predicts that high levels of interpersonal affection should generalize to produce decreased tendencies to use force in international relations. But ethnocentrism theory holds that high levels of ingroup affection will correspond with *increased* aggressive tendencies to use force toward outgroups in international relations.

A classic formulation of the inverse interpersonal generalization theory was Freud's:

It is always possible to bind together a considerable number of people in love, so long as there are other people left over to receive the manifestations of their aggressiveness. . . . When the Apostle Paul had postulated universal love between men as the foundation of his Christian community, extreme intolerance on the part of Christendom toward those who remained outside it became the inevitable consequence.[19]

Ethnocentrism theories are usually applied to groups as a whole. There are theorists in this tradition who would object to testing the validity of their ideas by looking only at differences between individuals within the professional elites of American government. These objections would be well taken: Theories of ethnocentrism come in rich and complex variety, and (as discussed below) there are at least some formulations which probably do apply collectively to the State Department.[20] Still, an inverse interpersonal generalization hypothesis does represent a reasonable formulation of the Freudian branch of ethnocentrism theory.

One element of ethnocentrism which probably holds more or less in general is national identification, the egocentric tendency to look out at the world from the perspective of (in this case) the United States. It is the subject's self-identification with his nation's overall foreign policy which allows the prediction of the specific policy differences that follow from personality differences. To give an obvious example: One statement of interpersonal generalization theory is that hostile Americans are more likely to advocate the use of force against the Soviet Union. A Soviet with the same trait would undoubtedly not favor such policies against his own country. Chapter 4 reports data that the men studied do identify with American foreign policy. Individual differences in this identification appear to be small—a result which is not surprising since the diplomats and the military officers have selected the implementation of such policy as their career.

A second statement of an ethnocentrism theory is that a man seeks to promote the values of his culture in his foreign policy recommendations. Democratic electoral processes, intellectual freedom, economic growth, and mass education are examples of values which American elites would be expected to wish to export. Although the State Department study did not explore this avenue, such ethnocentrism ("culturally-based idealism" is a less pejorative term) might well produce errors in judgment and not be obvious to the individuals making decisions.[21]

Deviations from Mental Health (a4)

A fourth theoretical tradition proposes that deviations from coopera- tive internationalism arise from traits many psychologists believe reflect poor mental health. Typical traits which have been studied and found to be associated in this way among the general public include: authoritarian- ism, dogmatism, neurotic conflict, low self-esteem, mistrust, low cognitive complexity, and intolerance of ambiguity.[22]

Many researchers in this tradition seem satisfied simply to demonstrate that bad goes with bad; empathetic explanations are few and far between. But, reading between the lines, the research suggests that men who are sus- picious of others, men who feel harassed or anxious or unsure of them- selves, or who have difficulty coping flexibly with complex situations are more likely to prefer policies whose meanings to them are strong, simple, and definitive. The majority of studies show deviations from mental health ideals leading to belligerent nationalism, but studies that have looked more carefully have also found that the same deviations may increase the likeli- hood that an individual will advocate a pacific isolationist withdrawal from international relations.

Herbert McClosky's work is illustrative of the best of this latter research. He studied a representative national sample of American citizens and a large number of delegates and alternates to the 1956 conventions of the Democratic and Republican parties. For both his mass and his political elite samples he concludes:

While (isolationism) is obviously a political attitude influenced by political circumstances, reference groups, demographic factors, and other such determinants, it is also shaped to a considerable extent by a complex set of personality variables, primarily of an aversive nature. Such personality states as misanthropy, psychological inflexibility, manifest anxiety, and low self-esteem have a powerful influence. . . . Although isolationism manifestly appears as a peaceful withdrawal from international entanglements and frequently has been interpreted as a simple desire to keep one's country from becoming militarily embroiled, it is characteristically xenophobic and belligerent in its posture toward foreign affairs. It represents, for the most part, a rejection of other men rather than a concern for them, a disavowal of responsibility and a strong urge to disengage oneself from obligations toward others.[23]

Two studies, one by Bernard Mennis and one by David Garnham, recently tested hypotheses from this tradition with foreign service officers.[24] Mennis interviewed 37 country desk officers and political assistants at the State Department and 58 military officers at the Defense Department who had responsibility for international political affairs. He found a significant (but low) relation between a composite measure of cognitive style (rigidity and dogmatism) and a composite measure of hard line anticommunism, nonsupport of arms control and disarmament, and verbal derogation of nonaligned nations. David Garnham conducted a similar study using a worldwide sample of 274 foreign service officers and found a significant (but low) relation between psychological flexibility and "world mindedness." However, both researchers also report that foreign service officers score very low on dogmatism and very high on psychological flexibility; thus it is unlikely that cases involving substantial consensus favorable to the use of force would be explained by dogmatism and personal rigidity. While these personality factors could (according to studies of the general public) produce hard-line policies in abundance if present, it appears to be a dynamic that is not engaged centrally in the decision of these elite groups to use force.

There is, however, a related theory I was interested in exploring. I had come increasingly to suspect that, as part of the normal process of socialization, many people experience themselves as *beneath* their government. Among the contents of the mind is the sense of one's self, one's subjective locus within the world imagined by the mind. Also within the mind is a vast collection of ideas and reified images, some of which are located for most people *above* their sense of themselves. Images located above the sense of self seem to include ideals and the *super*ego; and, of particular relevance here, the image of one's government and its foreign policy.

I suspected that this *political subordination,* the integration of the sense of self within a subjective hierarchical system, might produce systematic effects—among which are increased personal fear if American interests are threatened, an increased tendency toward self-assertive dominance of other nations to retain the status quo and American hegemony, and reduction in altruism and generosity.[25] I also suspected that there are men who, through *growing* up politically (i.e., dissolving the hierarchical structure between their sense of themselves and their image of government) would come to stand subjectively, in Goethe's phrase, *"above* the nations and to feel the good fortune or distress of his neighbor people as if it had happened to his own."[26] As a result of these conjectures, one deviation which the State Department study explores is the sense of political subordination of the self to government.

One additional factor studied in the "deviations from mental health" tradition has been mistrust. For example, Henry Kissinger, theorizing about the relation between domestic politics and foreign policy, argued that a low level of interpersonal trust was characteristic of Soviet leaders who lived through the Stalin period.[27] Consequently he proposed that Soviet leaders were unlikely to place more faith in the professed goodwill of the United States than the low trust they placed in their own colleagues .

The problem is of particular theoretical interest; if its effects can be captured by assessing individual differences within American foreign policy elites, it might identify one important and general influence of elite political culture on foreign policy. In addition the trait is an interesting object of study because Argyris's extensive social-psychological study of the State Department several years ago concluded that there were very *low* levels of interpersonal trust,[28] while Kissinger, in his article, implied that the opposite was true in the United States.

The Self in Organizational Context (a5)

Out of a desire for simplicity, much basic research on the linkage between personality and political attitudes has simply compared scores of personality scales with scores on political attitude scales. Such a straightforward effect may be the major story, but it does ignore the fact that individuals are seldom free-floating and responding only to a policy situation. Rather, they are embedded in a social context. And this social context includes, in this case, organizations with distinctive norms, operating styles, missions, self-images, philosophy, and viewpoint, and rewards for being successfully in the mainstream or appropriately creative in the service of the organization's mission, or sanctions for being too deviant, disruptive, or "far out."

A full treatment of this social context as it affects American foreign policy decision making would require an enormous amount of data and is far beyond the scope of the present investigation. But tests for some major sociological forces interacting with personality differences can be made. For example, I have tested the psychological effect of a sense of subordination of the self to American foreign policy (as described in the preceding section). It is also possible that an individual's group and organizational location may affect perspectives and mediate the effects of personality traits on policy attitudes. For this reason data from comparison groups at the Office of Management and Budget and the National War College will be used in two special tests to be described in the following chapters. First, there will be a test of whether group membership alone represents some significant difference in unmeasured forces, apart from personal predispositions, that are reflected in policy attitudes and perceptions. Second, there will be a test of whether group membership mediates the effects of personality differently within these different groups.

Numerous hypotheses could be generated about these interaction effects. But two seem especially relevant: first, that self-esteem will affect attitudes toward the use of force in interaction with an agency's specialty: high self-esteem diplomats should oppose force while high self-esteem military officers should support it more strongly, and self-esteem should have no effect among domestic policy specialists. Second, it will be possible to study whether personality engagement, as a general rule, is greater or less among FSOs and military officers compared with domestic policy specialists. The relationship, at this point, could be plausibly argued either way: one might say there will be a greater impact of emotional dynamics among national security professionals because these men are more ego-involved—foreign policy is more salient to them. Or one could argue, as Verba has suggested, that diplomats and military officers, as professionals, will have more rationally disciplined thinking in the national security area and their thinking will be *less* likely to exhibit systematic emotional influences.[29]

The Effects of Personality on Perception
Traditional theories of the effects of personality on the subject's perceptions of other nations have in general the same structure as the theories concerned with the effects of personality on policy. But there are a few differences, and a brief discussion of self-based inference, attribution of one's own subjective fantasy goals, and inverse self-based inference (b1, b2, and b3) will be useful.

Self-Based Inference (b1)
A major tradition of theorizing about the relation of personality to political perception has been self-based inference. Barber, for example, found that personality differences within local political elites in Connecticut produced different perceptions of the operation of their local political systems. Men who preferred close and intimate relations with others tended to believe decisions in their communities were made by a small group of men who discussed and planned their actions with one another. Men who preferred greater independence and psychological distance in interpersonal relations inferred that the leaders of their communities consulted widely in making decisions. Each man, then, tended to imagine decisions being made in his local community as he would make them if he held the central post.[30] Lane has suggested that such a process occurs generally: "Each of us is a model of man we use in our interpretation of others."[31] Herman Kahn has argued that this dynamic occurs in international political perceptions:

People tend to see the Russians in terms of their personalities: a bureaucratic and rigid type would see them as bureaucratic and rigid and an aggressive person would see them as aggressive. . . . You might sum it up by saying the right wing has an enemy . . . and the peace movement has a misguided friend.[32]

Attribution of Subjective Fantasy Goals (b2)

Men who are ambitious to feel active, strong, and powerful may imagine that Soviet leaders have the same ambitions, thus attributing their own strivings to others. (I list this dynamic separately here to retain the symmetry between the perception- and policy-traditions, but it seems parsimonious to simply expand the concept of "self" to include the attribution to others of one's dreams for an ideal self. In later chapters, therefore, I will use the general term "self-based inference" to include attribution to Soviet leaders of one's own dreams to become his ideal self (e.g., dreams of becoming active, strong, powerful)).

Inverse Self-Based Inference (b3)

There is an opposing epistemological tradition, that of inverse self-based inference. This tradition employs the Freudian concept of the projection of *repressed* impulses, proposing that the image of foreigners is constructed from an individual's impulses that are unacceptable to his conscious sense of himself. The Russians, in this formulation, would be the garbage heaps of an American's psyche, harbingers of brutal, savage, crude impulses a man would neither acknowledge in himself nor express toward his fellow Americans. Such a dynamic is part of the ethnocentrism syndrome, and as such has been proposed as the cause of perceptions that justify, and perhaps call forth, hostility against the Russians and other outgroups.

This ends our brief overview of theoretical traditions and research concerns. In the next chapter I will proceed to introduce the first of the two investigations, the State Department study.

3   The State Department Study: Descriptive Overview

To explore the psychology of foreign policy thinking among people engaged seriously in that enterprise, a random sample of 300 American foreign service officers stationed in Washington were invited to complete an extensive questionnaire assessing their personality traits, their foreign policy positions, and their perceptions. Forty-two percent of the people contacted agreed to provide data. The answers were provided in December, 1971, and January, 1972, just after an India-Pakistan war and before President Nixon's previously announced trip to Peking.[1]

In addition, to test theories that personality traits affect foreign policy thinking through interaction with organizational setting (a5, b5, chapter 2), data from two comparison groups were obtained: 49 mid-career military officers attending an advanced course at the National War College (now National Defense University) at Fort McNair in Washington, DC, and 39 domestic policy specialists at the Office of Management and Budget.[2]

The main purpose of this chapter is to outline key elements of the personality traits, images of reality, and foreign policy predispositions held by these men.[3] The questions and scales will be described, and part of the evidence reviewed for their relations with one another. Of special importance for later chapters will be the finding that high dominance, ambitious, competitive, and self-assertive people also tend to be mistrustful in their interpersonal relations and that people who advocate use of force in international relations also feel especially threatened by the Soviet Union. In other words, we shall see that *behavioral predispositions and images of reality vary together in consistent ways,* both in the interpersonal arena and in the international arena.

Background and Personality

Respondents came from all levels of the State Department (although there was a drop to 30% participation at the highest FSO-1 and 2 levels). The typical foreign service officer was well educated (M.A. degree), had served two to three tours of duty abroad, was in his early 40s.[4] The domestic affairs specialists were usually younger (late 20s and early 30s) with slightly more graduate education.[5] The military officers represented all services and were usually in their early 40s with 20 years of service, a B.A. degree, and some additional education since entering the military. Given their assignment to the National War College, they could be expected to move later into policy work involving political issues rather than to a field command.

A self-description of these men was provided by the Leary Interpersonal Checklist, an instrument developed by Dr. Timothy Leary before he left academic life for other pursuits. This consists of a series of 128 adjectives and adjectival phrases: the subject checks those he believes apply to himself. A scoring scheme allows one to arrive at measures of dominance-submission and affection-hostility.[6]

The subjects reported upon here accepted and rejected adjectives on the checklist that coalesce around four themes in their self-image. First, they are *independent,* especially in forming their attitudes and in thinking critically. Second, they *like responsibility.* Third, they *believe they are worthy men* (and further, they believe that they are so viewed by others). Finally, they think of themselves as *cordial* in their independence rather than as cool, aloof, or hostile.[7,8]

There are, of course, differences in the response patterns of the three groups. The military officers tend to be more dominant (checking forceful description like "stern but fair") than the civilians.[9] But one common characteristic, which will later help to explain the advocacy of military force, occurred in the percentage of men who checked "likes to compete." A majority of men in each group (53% at the State Department, 62% of domestic policy specialists, and 84% of military officers) said this was true about themselves.[10]

High self-regard and good mental health is indicated by two additional measures. The first is a measure of self-esteem. A man was asked to describe himself on a set of 7-interval adjective scales with evaluative connotations: good-bad, kind-cruel, skillful-bungling, honest-dishonest, friendly-menancing, and trusting-fearful. He was also asked to rate on these same scales the kind of person he would like to be, his ideal self. The gap between these two scores was taken as a measure of self-esteem—the greater the gap, the lower the self-esteem. The results show that these men believe themselves to live up very well to their own ideals: on the self-esteem scale (reverse scored and standardized from 0 to 10), the average in each group was between 8.6 and 9.0.[11,12]

A second indication of good mental health derived from a neuroticism scale in the Maudsley Personality Inventory. These six questions assess symptoms of internal conflict—difficulties in concentration (e.g., "My mind tends to wander even when I am trying to concentrate"), frequency of depression, and tendencies to pronounced mood swings. Men in all three groups scored very low (3.6 for diplomats on a scale of 0 to 10) and, compared with an average score of 5.1 obtained in a stratified random sample of 1,450 British adults, this suggests they are freer of ordinary internal conflict than an average citizen.[13]

These results also corroborate the research of Mennis and Garnham (described on p.13), who studied mental health in the State Department. Both men found remarkably low scores for psychological rigidity and dogmatism among foreign service officers, scores among the lowest on record.[14]

An important aspect of the psychology of these men is provided by ratings of how strong, active, and powerful they feel and would like to feel. Respondents described themselves and their ideal selves using adjective scales representing activity and power: active-passive, fast-slow, moving-still, strong-weak, hard-soft, tenacious-yielding, aggressive-defensive, leading-following, dominating-submitting, and resolute-irresolute. On a scale of 0 to 10 the average of these ratings for the self-image was 6.3 for domestic affairs specialists, 6.8 for diplomats and 7.6 for military officers. Thus, these men feel somewhat active and powerful now. *But almost all wish to feel stronger, more active, and more powerful:* the average desired level was 7.7 in the State Department with military officers being slightly higher, domestic affairs specialists slightly lower.[16] (This is an important result since, as we shall see, such personal dreams for strength, power, and activity shape both policy choices and inferences about the motivations of Russian leaders.) These results, which suggest that the typical diplomat is personally ambitious, corroborate the conclusion of Harr, who studied a 20% random sample of foreign service officers several years ago.[17]

Finally there are two additional personal characteristics of these men that have consequences for their foreign policy views. The first is interpersonal trust. Large majorities (from 68% to 88%) of men in each group said generally that "most people can be trusted," that people "would try to be fair," that they would "try to be helpful."[18,19] (These percentages average about 25% higher than answers given to these items by a random sample of American adults, who apparently have much less trust in human nature.)

A final trait (but one on which the subjects differ markedly) is how these men plan their own lives. Some men said they were simply "incrementalists," responding only to specific career opportunities as these arose. Other men were "long range planners" who set very definite long range goals for themselves and whose immediate choices were always subordinate to these long-term carrer goals. The State Department split about 50-50 between incrementalists and long range planners. But the comparison groups split in opposite ways; most domestic policy specialists were incrementalists (81%), most military officers (70%) were committed long range planners.[20,21] It will turn out (chapter 5), that these personal differences are significant in determining whether a man believes long range ambition motivates Soviet foreign policy behavior.

In summary, one can say that although there are differences between groups, the evidence from both self-descriptions and standard psychological tests converges to a consistent picture of these men. They are well educated and see themselves as intellectually independent. They have high self-esteem and are probably more mentally healthy than average. They describe themselves as friendly and assume the trustworthiness of other people (and are more inclined to do so than the average American adult). They feel active and personally powerful. Many like to compete with others. And they are ambitious: they want to feel stronger, more active, and more powerful than they do at present.[22]

Table 3.1 summarizes the correlations among selected personality scales for the FSO random sample. Included with other test results are dominance-submission, hostility-affection, and introvert-extravert scales on which the groups did not differ substantially and where the scores tended to be near the theoretical midpoint.[23] The table confirms Eckhardt's summary of studies of the general public (see note 16 to chapter 2), that there is a tendency for different facets of the willful assertion of the self to go together: dominant people tend to be slightly more hostile,

Table 3.1

Inter-Scale Correlations of Selected Personality Traits, FSO Sample

	1	2	3
1 Dominance	1.00		
2 Hostility	.325***	1.00	
3 Likes to Compete	.450***	.350***	1.00
4 Extraversion	.403***	.200*	.261**
5 Trust	.013	−.343***	−.157
6 Long Range Life Planning	.254***	.076	.183*
7 Self-Esteem	.182*	−.019	.004
8 Self: Activity/Power	.606***	.471***	.456***
9 Ideal Self: Activity/Power	.334***	.385***	.454***

* = p < .05   ** = p < .01   *** = p < .001

Neurotic conflict does not correlate significantly with any of the traits.

For entries in this table, *N* is between 112 and 126.

The *p*-value is the likelihood that the correlation could result from random processes.

Correlations (*r*'s) in the table can range from −1 (perfect negative correlation) to 0 (no correlation) to +1 (perfect positive correlation).

4	5	6	7	8
1.00				
.005	1.00			
.052	.010	1.00		
.041	.099	.010	1.00	
.440***	−.127	.232**	.308***	1.00
.337***	−.206*	.086	.076	.668***

like to compete, are more extraverted, feel more powerful, are more ambitious, and are more oriented to long range career planning. Men who are
ambitious and hostile are also significantly more mistrustful of others. This
same pattern of correlations appeared when all groups were considered together.

Views of the World

In this section I will sketch main themes in the perceptions of the world
held by those elites. In the following section I will summarize common
themes in the foreign policy decision-making area.

What beliefs and perceptions do these FSOs hold? Let us begin with
views of the Soviet Union. FSOs tend to hold, either moderately or
strongly, a traditional view of the origins of the Cold War. They believe
that in the late 1940s the USSR had substantial expansionist ambitions
and would have "sought to extend itself into every nook and cranny in
Western Europe were it not checked." Almost all reject, on balance, the
idea that the Soviet Union was only *reacting* in those years, i.e., that
"Soviet conflict with the West arose from dangers to Soviet national security emanating from the Western powers. Soviet foreign policy was neither
hostile nor expansionist but was misperceived by the West in this way."
On a scale of 0 to 10 (10 being strongly traditional) diplomats scored a
mean of 8.1. Military officers were almost all strongly traditional (9.1);
domestic policy specialists were on the traditional side too (7.1), although
less exclusively.[24]

Soviet foreign policy was rated by these men on the same series of
adjective scales listed on p. 19. On the scale of "friendly-menacing," men
in all three groups agreed that Soviet foreign policy at the time of the
study was, on average, slightly to moderately menacing (between 6.5 and
7.1 on a scale of 0 to 10).[25] They were concerned and vigilant, but far
from being terrified of Soviet r uclear capabilities and intentions.

Beliefs about Soviet foreign policy were also assessed concretely by pre-
senting a series of eight options to describe major Soviet foreign policy objectives in the Middle East. These options ranged from "they really don't
know what they want" (5.6% of FSOs believed this) to a belief in major
Soviet expansionist ambitions: "Their involvement is part of a long range

plan to establish influence across North Africa, to turn the Mediterranean
into a Soviet lake, and thereby to intimidate our European allies in
NATO." Fifty-nine percent of FSOs believed this was true. (Sixty-three
percent of the military officers agreed, but only 38% at OMB.)[26]

A final element in diplomats' beliefs about the Soviet Union was that
Soviet-American relations have improved in the long run and that the
United States was more secure in 1972 than in the early days of the cold
war. Asked to compare American national security today with its national
security in 1954, diplomats (and domestic policy specialists), by a ratio of
3:2, said our national security had increased. However, in the sharpest
disagreement recorded in this study, military officers strongly believed the
reverse: by a ratio of almost 5:1 they saw a decline.[27]

The surface reason for different national security judgements was
straightforward. Those who saw a national security increase cited psychological factors: the increased experience of US and USSR leaders in dealing
with each other, the better international climate, greater trust and mutual
understanding. Those who saw a national security decrease cited military
factors: the great increase, since 1954, in Soviet strategic nuclear capability relative to that of the United States, as well as weakening domestic support for a strong American foreign policy, and (for some) the "naively
liberal" views of international relations taught in colleges and universities.

Finally, each man was asked to locate his view of "the course of world
politics in the years to come" along a scale between two scenarios. One
scenario sketched a future that was "hopeful, even reassuring;" the other
scenario sketched a future which was "grim, even frightening":

A. The prospects for the course of world politics in the years to come are
hopeful, even reassuring. Developing agreements for the control of nuclear
weapons and a growing awareness of the destructiveness of even limited
war suggest a new sobriety and maturity. Rising educational levels among
elites of both developed and underdeveloped states, a growing awareness
of shared destiny, and negotiations among important powers on their
major substantive disagreements suggest that negotiation and cooperation
rather than military conflict will characterize future trends. Long range
programs to deal with emerging problems of population and resource constraints can be expected to move into high gear in the light of growing
consensus of their necessity.

B. The prospects for the course of world politics in the years to come are grim, even frightening. The expansion of nuclear arsenals by the super-powers and by China, and the growing size and far-flung deployment of Soviet naval power heighten the chances of military conflict and the potential destructiveness of that conflict if it should get out of hand. The growing military capabilities of underdeveloped states, together with heightened national consciousness, suggest that war between some of them is not to be unexpected—the pressures from the population explosion and natural resource constraints make such conflict even more likely.

On a 10-point scale (10 being "grim, even frightening") diplomats scored at a mean of 3.9, military officers at 4.0, and domestic policy specialists at 3.3. Splitting the scale at the midpoint shows the consensus explicitly: 65% of American diplomats predict fair weather in the years ahead: 61% of military officers and 73% of domestic affairs specialists also agree.[28]

In summary, then, American diplomats tend to believe that the traditional cold war perceptions of Soviet conduct were accurate; they see our national security as having increased over the years; they see the Soviet Union as slightly to moderately menacing, with marked expansionist desires in the Middle East. But on balance they are optimistic and believe that American foreign policy will cope well with Soviet foreign policy challenges and other problems in the years ahead. In all, they see a "hopeful, even reassuring" future before us.

Attitudes and Policy Judgments

What of the attitudes and policy thinking of these men? Key elements clustered in seven themes.

I. America should become more internationalist.

The questionnaire asked; "Some people believe that America should seek in the long run to negotiate mutually acceptable international agreements whereby all nations will begin to turn over at least some elements of national sovereignty to an internationally elected body. Other people oppose this idea. Do you believe America should try to develop international political institutions of this kind or should we retain our national sovereignty?"

Seventy-three percent of the diplomats checked "Move toward stronger international political institutions." Slight majorities of the two other groups (56% of domestic policy specialists and 54% of military officers) also selected this option.[29] (Judging by the lack of administration initiative in this area it is probably true that most diplomats were—and would be still—ahead of current foreign policy in their desire to create stronger world institutions.)

A desire for greater involvement with other nations was also evidenced in answers to questions about economic assistance. Diplomats favored a significant increase in economic foreign aid—to about $4.8–5.0 billion annually. This figure is less than the 1% of the GNP optimistically called for by the Pearson Commission.[30] Still, diplomats desired to provide more aid than at present; and they placed moderately strong importance on it (7.1 on a scale of 0 to 10). However, they opposed the high level of foreign arms sale and military aid characteristic of the Nixon administration. Most wanted a cap of about $1 billion and many would have liked to shift exclusively to sales and away from grants. (Military officers, as might be expected, were much more favorable to military aid and attached stronger importance to it.)[31]

It is notable, as well, that diplomats and men in other groups also believed that the greater part of American economic aid should be channeled primarily through international institutions: 60% of diplomats wanted more routing through international institutions; 62% of domestic policy specialists and 58% of military officers agreed.[32]

2. America should place high priority on preventing unprovoked international aggression.

Each man was asked to rank his relative priority for eight American foreign policy objectives in underdeveloped countries. These goals and their average ranking (on a scale of 0 to 10) are listed in table 3.2.

A notable consensus was the high priority for "a government which will not engage in unprovoked aggression against other nations." This high ranking (higher even than given "A government which is neutral or pro-American in its foreign policy" (no. 5 of the table)) may be simply a manifestation of the prevalent ideology in a status quo power, but I suspect it also represents an achievement in civilization. Its high priority probably

Table 3.2

Desired American Policy Priorities in Underdeveloped Countries, FSO Sample

1. A government that will not engage in unprovoked aggression against other nations	7.26
2. A government with broad popular support	7.22
3. A stable government capable of preserving internal order	6.10
4. A government which maintains civil liberties	5.42
5. A government which is neutral or pro-American in its foreign policy	5.17
6. Rapid economic development	5.12
7. A government which allows broad opportunities for American business investment	2.01
8. A government which retains the free enterprise system	1.31

Theoretical range 0 to 10 with 10 being the highest relative priority. N = 124.
SD (SE): 1. 3.63 (.33); 2. 2.73 (.25); 3. 2.64 (.24); 4. 2.51 (.23); 5. 2.75 (.25);
6. 2.84 (.26); 7. 3.49 (.31); 8. 2.09 (.19).

reflects a strong, civilized, superego injunction against aggression in general.

In history there has not always been this principled opposition to aggression. What is important to note is that a moral (and/or political) injunction against "aggression" may now be offered as one explanation of the use of force in current American foreign policy, a use of force which is seen as a *response* to disruptive events, an effort to preserve and protect the stability, security, and peace of the world by establishing and maintaining the principle that changes initiated by military aggression will not succeed.

The comparison groups agreed in giving a high rank to preventing aggression (7.4 at OMB, 6.4 at NWC), but they split strongly in other ways that seem to reflect a conservative-liberal dimension.[33] Military officers give their highest priority to maintaining order in underdeveloped countries (8.01) and care about this more than about broad popular support (6.10) or about civil liberties (5.09). Domestic policy specialists, however, give much higher priority to broad popular support (7.98) and to civil liberties (7.37); they do not place high value on stable governments (5.6), and they are relatively indifferent (compared to both FSOs and military officers) to whether an underdeveloped country's foreign policy favors Communist interests (3.3).[34]

In section 7 of this chapter evidence will be presented regarding the tendency of these men to advocate the use of military force in different scenarios. There it will become clear that perceived Communist *aggression* is a major stimulus to which many of these men would respond with the use of force. But there is evidence that communism *itself* is not the key objection of these men. The questionnaire asked:

Some people say that Communist governments which are nationalist and nonexpansionist should be acceptable to the United States and that we should not try to oppose the emergence of such governments in underdeveloped countries. Other people say that communism is objectionable in itself and argue that the United States should work against the emergence of such governments in underdeveloped countries, even if they pose no military threat to us or our allies. How do you believe the United

States should respond to the possible development of nationalist, non-expansionist Communist governments in underdeveloped countries?

Subjects were to check one of two options: "Accept it if it happens; do not try to oppose it" or "Oppose it." Eighty percent of American diplomats checked the "Accept it if it happens" box. Ninety-seven percent of domestic policy specialists and 69% of the military officers felt the same way.[35]

In other words, an ideologically crusading anticommunism apparently had waned among the professional mid-elites of American government by 1972. There was openness to détente. *If* the Communist world was willing to be pragmatic and "live and let live," then so were almost all of these men.

3. The export and promotion of capitalism and "free enterprise" should receive low priority in foreign policy.
This view, counter to what a Marxist would maintain is true of American elite beliefs, is shown by very low rankings accorded to objectives 7 and 8 (table 3.2): "A government which allows broad opportunities for American business investment" and "A government which retains the free enterprise system." These priorities were at the bottom of the list.

A similar belief that business interests should be subordinate to political control was shown by the answer to the question:

Suppose you were asked by the Secretary of State whether the United States should take the initiative, now, in developing international political institutions to govern the functioning of multinational business corporations. What would be your attitude toward such initiatives?

All groups favored such initiatives: 72% of diplomats, 53% of domestic policy specialists, and 61% of military officers would recommend that international business be subordinate to stronger multinational political controls.[36] These men tended to be ahead (if that is the correct word) of recent American administrations in their low deference to business interests. (It seems plausible that such interests carry more weight at political levels than among career professionals.)

4. American foreign policy is a friendly, moral force for good in the world.
This finding is based on adjective ratings for both American foreign policy

and ideal American foreign policy along the evaluative dimensions listed
on p. 19. American foreign policy was rated quite positively. The gap between the actual and ideal images was used as a measure of the idealization
of current American foreign policy (the greater the gap the lower the idealization): reverse-scored on a scale of 0 to 10, FSOs score at an average of
8.2 (military officers, 8.1; domestic policy specialists, 7.2). There was a
virtuous image of the nation, and substantial approval of what was perceived as the benevolence and friendliness of American foreign policy.[37]

*5. Its present 1½-war military capability is adequate for the challenges
America faces in the world.*
At the time of the study official American policy was a "1½ war" capability level—"1" being the capability necessary for one major war, "½" being
the capability necessary for one small war. Diplomats scored exactly at 1.5
as their desired capability level; military officers wanted some increase (1.7),
domestic affairs specialists wanted a slight further decrease (1.3).[38]

*6. American foreign policy should become more activist and powerful in
shaping the world.*
Each man rated his image of the activity and power of American foreign
policy using adjective scales upon which he rated himself and his ideal
self (p. 20). American foreign policy was ranked as somewhat active and
powerful by diplomats (6.3 on a 0 to 10 scale). Domestic policy specialists
and military officers agreed with this view although their perceptions were
slightly lower (5.7 and 5.6).[39] Yet *all groups agreed they wanted America
to be more activist and powerful* with group means for this image between
7.0 and 7.9.[40] We have already seen other evidence of these activist desires
in the earlier discussion of international political institutions, negotiated
controls on multinational business, more economic aid (and, for the military officers, more military aid).

*7. The use of American military force is necessary or desirable in certain
situations.*
Each man gave policy recommendations in five scenarios close to actual
situations in American foreign policy. These scenarios and the percentage
of men who advocated the use of force are listed in table 3.3.[41]

Table 3.3

Use-of-Force Scenarios, by Group

	Percent Advocating Force		
	OMB	FSO	NWC
1 Bay of Pigs[a]	36.1	49.6	79.6
2 Vietnam[b]	36.1	64.8	83.3
3 Soviet Union-Caribbean Buildup[c]	58.3	71.0	79.6
4 Indonesia[d]	11.1	16.8	24.5
5 Dominican Republic[e]	27.8	13.6	51.0
Mean Percent of Cases[f]	33	42.9	63.3

Actual questions were:

1. *Bay of Pigs:* "Suppose that you had known of the plans for the Cuban Bay of Pigs invasion shortly before it occurred and you believed it could succeed in replacing the Castro regime. What would have been your view of the invasion at that time?"

2. *Vietnam:* "Suppose that during the middle 1960s you believed that the American military involvement in Vietnam would succeed in all of its announced objectives by the end of 1968. What would have been your attitude toward this involvement at that time?"

3. *Soviet Union-Caribbean:* "Suppose that the Soviet Union in the next few years begins a large scale naval buildup in the Caribbean. It becomes clear that only the threat or use of force can reverse the buildup. What would be your attitude toward this alternative?"

4. *Indonesia:* "Suppose that in the early 1960s you believed that President Sukarno's move to the left would shortly result in a military alliance between Indonesia and Communist China. If you also believed that an American military intervention could replace the Sukarno government by a pro-American or neutralist government, what would have been your attitude toward such an intervention?"

5. *Dominican Republic:* "Suppose you were called upon to give advice just prior to President Johnson's dispatch of American troops to the Dominican Republic. Suppose you believed that dispatching the troops would help to prevent bloodshed and stabilize the domestic politics of the Dominican Republic—but you did not believe there was a threat of a Communist takeover. What would have been your attitude toward sending in American troops?"

Original responses were to 7-point Likert scales. Tabled percents are of those checking one of the three advocacy positions. Ns were 36 or 37 (OMB), 125 or 126 (FSO), 48 or 49 (NWC).

[a] p(OMB-FSO) ns, p(FSO-NWC) $< .0006$, p(OMB-NWC) $< .0001$.

[b] p(OMB-FSO) $< .004$, p(FSO-NWC) $< .03$, p(OMB-NWC) $< 3 \times 10^{-5}$.

[c] p(OMB-FSO) and p(FSO-NWC) ns, p(OMB-NWC) $< .06$.

[d] All intergroup differences ns.

[e] p(OMB-FSO) $< .04$, p(FSO-NWC) $< 7 \times 10^{-7}$, p(OMB-NWC) $< .05$.

[f] Standard deviations: 27.6 (OMB), 25.0 (FSO), 25.3 (NWC). p(OMB-FSO) $< .04$, p(FSO-NWC) $< 3 \times 10^{-6}$, p(OMB-NWC) $< 2 \times 10^{-6}$. Single case significance levels determined by χ^2, df = 1, Yates correction where appropriate.

As discussed in chapter 2, the evidence shows that the specific situation is the major determinant of whether force will be used. The advocacy of force varied widely—from 71% of diplomats in the case of a Soviet naval buildup in the Caribbean, to 13.6% of diplomats in a modified version of President Johnson's Dominican Republic decision. The major situational determinant appears to be perceived *threat,* particularly the dramatic expansion of Communist influence involving military force. Still, there is often significant disagreement within groups and also between groups, with military officers being more likely advocates of the use of force than civilians, and FSOs more likely to employ force than domestic policy specialists.

I also collected data on how *strongly* a man would advocate the use of force in each of these cases. Diplomats often recommend the use of force even when they are not strongly committed emotionally (they show an average emotional intensity of only 1.8 on a 3-point scale). This reflects the fact, I think, that they are professionals, accustomed to making decisions with some degree of personal detachment. (Such professionalism was reflected by a member of the State Department's Policy Planning Staff who characterized President Johnson's dispatch of troops to the Dominican Republic to me as a "surgical intervention.") I think this also means they will advocate the use of force (and, implicitly, the possible death of American soldiers) without actually being willing to die, themselves, to see the objective achieved.[42]

Does this element of professional detachment increase or decrease the likelihood of war? I think it cuts both ways. Shutting off emotions could produce the use of force at a lower threshold of emotional commitment. On the other hand such detachment could allow men to react more calmly and dispassionately to international situations, thereby reducing the likelihood of the use of force, and it could modify a man's involvement so he will be satisfied to achieve limited political ends rather than total victory. On balance, I tentatively believe that professional detachment in the State Department has the second effect: I base this guess on the evidence in the next two chapters which show the greater tendency of military officers to advocate force arises, in part, because they are more involved emotionally in their foreign policy views.

Let me add, as a footnote, that while at the State Department I was told of the work of another researcher who had asked diplomats favoring the Vietnam War when they "had first begun to believe war was a legitimate instrument of national policy." Men I talked with were offended at being asked such a question. Some supported the Vietnam War but they did *not* believe "war was a legitimate instrument of national policy." Instead they felt that "using force" was an unpleasant "necessity." To my ear this legalism sounded like a sophisticated mental operation designed to retain a moral self-image by splitting off inhibiting moral considerations from practical ones. If so, then it could mark a significant fact that many foreign service officers are not completely comfortable with the idea of using military force even when advocating it—a possibility that I will raise in more detail later in a discussion of FSO modal personality and ambivalence.

Relations Between Selected Policy Attitudes and Perceptions

Table 3.4 summarizes the correlations between selected policy attitudes and perceptions in the FSO random sample. I have included in the list results of an additional item assessing a man's domestic political views; on a self-report scale (rescaled here from 0 to 10 with 10 being highly conservative) diplomats were on the liberal side (3.45), OMB professionals were there more so (2.89), while military officers were on the conservative side (6.12).[43]

The most striking relation in the table is the organizing role apparently played by the belief that strong Soviet expansionist ambitions lay behind and motivated Soviet conduct in the early years of the cold war: FSO traditionalists were more inclined to use force, to desire greater military capability, and to see current Soviet foreign policy as expansionist. There is a syndrome of fear, suspicion, and militaristic tendencies. (Or, to put it differently, an interconnection among relative trust of the Soviet Union, approval of lower levels of war capability, and a disinclination to use force.) There is, indeed, a tendency for men to be, psychologically, either "hawks" or "doves," and to adopt the postures, in any particular case, that express this internal psychological coherence. This same pattern of relationships emerged even more strongly when all groups were considered together.[44]

What is crucial to note about these patterns is that *perceptual differ-ences and policy differences tend to go together* across disparate situations, reflecting (as we shall see in the next two chapters) systematic *personal predispositions* to be either mistrustful and tough or sanguine and opposed to military emphases. Claiming to be speaking objectively about reality and how to deal with it (and believing sincerely that this is what they are doing), hawks, doves, and those in between will be seen to be partly offer-ing mere rationalizations of predispositions.

Summary

In sum, these men believe America is a beneficent force in the world; they wish it to become more activist in providing economic aid (but reducing military aid), more activist in seeking to develop stronger international po-litical institutions generally, and specifically more active in controlling the multinational corporations; they believe America should use military force in certain selected situations, especially to establish the norm that unpro-voked aggression and international disorder will not be tolerated; they are receptive to the idea of detente in principle, and they agree with America's present level of military capability. A crude comparison with recent Amer-ican foreign policy suggests that the State Department is the home of more enthusiasm for building international political institutions, less deference to business, more support for economic assistance, and less support for military assistance than the top political elites in Washington. Such find-ings are also evidence for the candor of the men who agreed to participate.

(Yet it is possible that the actual rate of private disagreement in the State Department is somewhat understated by these data. One of the un-pleasant lessons I learned while conducting research in Washington was that there are some grown men who live in such fear of retaliation, disap-proval, and rejection by their superiors that they do not feel comfortable to express an independent judgment even in private. It is not just in for-eign countries that people can feel so intimidated that they forgo the exer-cise of basic human rights.)

Besides reporting the responses and establishing their plausibility, this

Table 3.4

Intercorrelations of Selected Policy Items and Perceptions, FSO Sample

	1	2	3
1 Use of Force in General	1.00		
2 Force—Bay of Pigs	.660***	1.00	
3 Force—Vietnam	.619***	.369***	1.00
4 Domestic Conservatism	.395***	.303***	.258***
5 Soviet Foreign Policy "Menace"	.139	.026	.180
6 Traditional Cold War Origins	.337***	.299***	.321***
7 Soviet Expansionist Wishes, Middle East	.292***	.281***	.116
8 Force Capability Desired	.122	204*	.232**
9 Acceptance of Nonexpansionist Communist Governments	−.191	−.279**	−.101

*p < .05   **p < .01   ***p < .001

For entries in this table, N is between 122 and 126.

4	5	6	7	8
1.00				
−.011	1.00			
.262**	.155	1.00		
.101	.086	.302***	1.00	
.134	−.005	.327***	.155	1.00
−.157	−.236**	−.085	−.083	.003

chapter has introduced the correlations within (1) personality organization and (2) the organization of foreign policy action and perception, showing that there is a syndrome linking both power-seeking and power-assertion (or their opposites) with beliefs about the threatening (or reassuring) nature of other people or other nations.[45] In chapters 4 and 5, I turn to the task of testing the possible causal effects of the personal syndrome on foreign policy action and perception.

4   Foreign Policy as Self-Expression

The secret title of any book is "how to be more like me."

Anonymous

In this chapter I undertake three tasks: First, I will test the relevance of the five traditional theories summarized in chapter 2 for identifying the effects of personal emotional predispositions on foreign policy choices; second, I will describe the policy tendencies and internal ambivalences that tend to be created by the modal personality of these mid-elite respondents; and third, I will present a summary theory that major foreign policy decisions are crucially the personal self-expression of the policy maker, the view that "what you decide depends ultimately on who you are."

What the data analysis in this chapter does is to match each man's personality trait score with his policy attitude score. Such matching can be represented by points on a graph; this allows a researcher to view the results for all of the men taken together. A "best fit" straight line is put through the scatter of points, and its slope describes directly the relation between scores: a line which slopes upward (positive) shows that an increase in the personality trait score tends to be associated with (causes) a higher attitude score.[1] When the slope of the line is downward (negative) it shows that an increase in the personality trait score is associated with (causes) a lower attitude score. In this chapter we will be concerned primarily with two policy attitude scores: the percentage of the five scenarios in which a man advocated the use of force (0% to 100%), and the "number of wars" capability a man wanted America to maintain (from ½ to 2½).

For readers familiar with the mathematics used to compare scores and derive descriptive equations, I have placed details of the best-fit equations in appendixes A and B. In the text I will simply summarize their main features, and describe how these equations are to be read.

A best-fit equation is of the straight-line form $Y = a_0 + b_1 X$, where Y is the dependent (policy) score, a_0 is a constant term which is the estimated value of Y when an individual scores at 0 (the lowest score) on the value of X (the personality trait score).[2] The term b_1, a derived coefficient, is the slope of the line. A positive value of b_1 means the line slopes upward (as the score on the personality trait X increases by 1 unit there tends to be a shift of b_1 units upward in the Y score). A negative b_1 means that the line slopes downward, so that people who score higher on X tend to have lower scores on Y.

Two important summary numbers in the tables in appendix B are R^2 and $p(F)$. R^2 is a number between 0 and 1 which tells how tightly the points cluster around the line. If R^2 equals 1, this implies that the difference in X scores are the sole cause of differences in Y scores; if R^2 is low it means that changes in Y are affected by many forces other than simply the X being considered. In every case in this chapter and the next, R^2 will be low—showing that a single personality trait is only one element in a complex set of other personality traits and situational and other factors that enter into the policy decisions in any specific case.

Another way to say this is that b_1 estimates the impact of a different decision maker (different on only this trait) if everything else were held constant.[3] R^2 estimates the size of the other factors that have to be held constant in order for this estimate to be accurate.

The final important number is $p(F)$. It is relevant because scores sometimes can vary together due to the happenstance of random processes, and this possibility must be known to be small before an equation can be taken seriously. The $p(F)$ estimate is the probability that the equation estimate could be produced by random fluctuations rather than by real effects.[4] A typical statement for an equation in this study would be "$p(F) < .001$," which means that there is less than one chance in a thousand that the derived equation could have resulted if the subjects had simply written down their choices for X and Y at random.[5] Thus we can have confidence that we are viewing real relationships.

The tables and resultant equations set forth in appendix B are slightly more complex than the foregoing. This is because the study allowed for the possibility that the different groups might have best-fit lines that differed from one common line. It also allowed for the possibility that other unexpressed differences between groups might make for different propensities in policy attitudes between groups. Significant slope shifts for the National War College (NWC) or Office of Management and Budget (OMB) are noted. Significantly different constant terms for NWC or OMB are expressed as intercept shifts for each group.

As noted in chapter 2, a characteristic assumed for these men was their personal identification with American foreign policy. This assumption, a basis for the specific predictions of later theories, was confirmed by a comparison of the images these men held of American foreign policy and their images of themselves provided by the adjective rating scales with evaluative and activity-power connotations discussed earlier.[6] The image of American foreign policy was close to the self-image and differences in self-image were associated with corresponding differences in the image of American foreign policy.[7]

Let me now turn to evaluating my results in terms of the five traditional theories listed in chapter 2: (a1) interpersonal generalization, (a2) displacement of subjective fantasy goals, (a3) ethnocentrism and inverse interpersonal generalization, (a4) defects in mental health, and (a5) the interaction of personality and organizational setting.

Personality Effects on Policy

Interpersonal Generalization (a1)

The first theory considered in chapter 2 was interpersonal generalization. Confirming findings of the present study are that the advocacy of military force will be greater among those whose personalities are characterized by:

1. Greater *interpersonal hostility* among military officers, and possibly among diplomats. However, there is no correlation among domestic policy professionals.[8] (I will turn later in this chapter to this problem of different strengths of personality-trait engagement in different groups.)

2. *Liking to compete with others* among diplomats and military officers. (In this case only, the Soviet Union scenario is omitted from the analysis, since a further breakdown showed that the relation held only for the four small-country scenarios.)

As already mentioned, R^2 was low (here, about .15) for any single personality-measure equation. In other words, there is no single answer to the problem of war, no single personality trait which, like a bolt of lightning, illuminates the entire landscape. Rather, each equation adds one piece to the puzzle and, while the explanatory power of personality traits in the aggregate will be substantial, the evidence is clear that these are complex men and complex situations, with subtle themes woven into the tapestry of their decision processes.

These first results support interpersonal generalization theory, but the vanishing effect of interpersonal competition in the case of possible confrontation with the Soviet Union ($r = -.0069$ for all subjects combined) suggests an important subtlety: men who enjoy competition are inclined to assert dominance in small countries but to hold this predisposition in check when faced with a possible direct confrontation by the Soviet Union.

There are also group-based interactions reflected in different positive slopes of the best-fit lines. My summary has emphasized the upper end of these lines (e.g., that more interpersonally hostile and aggressive military officers are more likely to advocate the use of force). G. K. Chesterton's famous sleuth, Father Brown, once warned against being too hasty by looking only in the direction a stick was pointing. "The other end of the stick," he commented, "always points the opposite way."[9] This caveat applies to the interpretation of these lines: that the interpersonal hostility line is more steeply positive among military officers does mean that hostile military officers are more predisposed than hostile diplomats to advocate the use of force—but the military line is not only steeper going *up*, it is steeper going *down* as well; a friendly military officer is more likely to oppose the use of force, for this reason, than is a friendly diplomat. The steeper line tells us that military officers are more *emotionally engaged* in making their policy recommendations.

Interpersonal generalization also helps to explain the desired level of war capability. Greater war capability levels are desired by:

1. More interpersonally hostile and competitive military officers (but there is no discernible effect of these personality traits among civilians).

2. The *less* dominant domestic policy specialists. In other words, the more dominant a domestic policy specialist at OMB, the more he wants to cut military spending.

Displacement of Subjective Fantasy Goals (a2)
A man's ambitious dreams, his excursions into his Walter Mitty fantasy life, directly affect his predisposition to use force (although not the level

of war capability desired). In all groups a greater desire to feel active and powerful increases the predisposition to advocate the use of military force. The emotional engagement of this dimension is stronger among military officers than among diplomats, and weakest among domestic policy professionals.

A possible reason for this finding is suggested by studies conducted by Kite and by Schlenker and Tedeschi.[10] They report that subjects in experiments who used coercion to produce change *felt more powerful* than did subjects who used rewards to produce change, even though the experimenters manipulated events so that the subjects in both groups actually produced equal amounts of change. The evidence (there and here) suggests that there is a visceral logic which ties feeling powerful more readily to the use of the stick than to the use of the carrot.

But the issue also arises whether ambitious men might advocate the use of force in a specific organizational context because they sense, at least unconsciously, that such policies might further their own careers. This would not be the complete story here—domestic policy specialists, who would have no reason to expect promotion or professional visibility from being hard-line in their foreign policy views, show the same behavior, although to a diminished extent. But it may be a *part* of the story at the State Department and especially among military officers—although among military officers there is a tendency generally to be more emotionally engaged in foreign policy issues on a number of dimensions, and the heightened impact of personal ambition is not unique, among all of the factors considered in this chapter, in its greater engagement.

Ethnocentrism and Inverse Interpersonal Generalization (a3)

So far the evidence has established straightforward interpersonal generalization (rather than inverse generalization) as the major story among these men. There was one exception—at OMB dominant men wanted lower military spending, but in the absence of additional evidence for an ethnocentrism syndrome shown in intra-elite personality differences, it seemed more realistic to interpret this correlation as an interaction of personality with the role of being centrally concerned with domestic programs.

However, a second set of tests can be conducted to see whether the tendency to idealize group characteristics (in this case, American foreign policy) is associated with greater hostility and aggression toward other nations. There was only one significant correlation: at OMB the tendency to advocate force was positively related to the idealization of American foreign policy. Thus it may be that these men on the periphery of foreign policy are characterized by personality-based ethnocentrism. But this conclusion is more likely spurious: we saw in chapter 3 that men at OMB tended to be lower in their idealization of American foreign policy (they were more disillusioned by it). Thus the observed correlation probably tells us only that the "low" end of the ethnocentrism line is true—that disillusionment with government policy and opposition to military force go together. There is no evidence that those professionals with high levels of national pride are more hostile to other nations. On the contrary, as the evidence reported on p. 26 suggests, these men, even those who would use force, are internationalists.

Defects in Mental Health (a4)

The questionnaire was designed to explore four traits reflecting interpersonal relations and mental health: neurotic symptons, trust, self-esteem, and political transcendence.

The first of these traits, the score on the Maudsley inventory of intrapsychic conflict, shows:

1. A greater incidence of internal conflict increases a predisposition to be either a stronger *advocate* or a stronger *opponent* of the use of force than average.

2. Among military officers, a greater incidence of internal conflict produces only a greater tendency to use force.

These results, in agreement with earlier research (see chapter 2) suggest that internal conflict leads a man to prefer simple, definitive modes of dealing with the world; he becomes more strongly militarist *or* antimilitarist. The evidence also suggests that the organizational setting affects which direction is chosen, so that among military officers the more internally conflicted are more likely to adopt a hardline stance.

The comparison between interpersonal trust scores and scores for the use of force and desired military capability shows:

1. The greater the interpersonal trust, the greater the reluctance to use force.[11,12]

2. At OMB, and perhaps at State and NWC, greater interpersonal trust leads a man to favor lower levels of military capability.[13]

The next significant set of causal effects involve self-esteem:

1. High self-esteem diplomats (and to an even greater extent, high self-esteem men at OMB) *oppose* the use of force. But high self-esteem military officers are much more likely to *advocate* military responses.

2. High self-esteem diplomats and high self-esteem OMB respondents favor a *higher* war capability. But high self-esteem military officers favor a *lower* war capability.[14]

The first result appears straightforward: high self-esteem civilians believe more confidently in nonmilitary approaches, high self-esteem military officers place more confidence in military approaches. The second result apparently means that high self-esteem civilians, while less likely to use force, also want a "big stick" available if the necessity to use it arises. High self-esteem military officers may be expressing pride in the competence of the American military and believe the job can be done with the present 1½ war capability.[15]

Finally, political transcendence (of psychological subordination to American foreign policy) shows systematic causal effects:

l. The greater the political transcendence, the greater the opposition to the use of force (a tendency which may be slightly stronger at OMB).

2. The greater the political transcendence, the lower the war capability desired.

A further exploration showed additional effects of political transcendence. It increases (in all groups) the relative priority for rapid economic development in underdeveloped countries, reduces (in all groups and especially at OMB) the concern for maintaining neutral or pro-American governments, and (at OMB) leads a man to care more strongly about promoting civil liberties.

In short, political transcendence does seem to catalyze a "neighborly" state of mind: men become less drawn to coercion, become more generous and altruistic in the policies they would advocate, less likely to require non-Communist governments in the underdeveloped world.[16]

Relative Impact of Various Personality Traits and (a5) the Organizational Setting

Table 4.1 summarizes the expected impact of the personality traits studied on the advocacy of force. This is the difference in the percentage of cases in which force is advocated that would be predicted to result, all other things being equal, if a man scoring "0" on a personality trait were replaced by a man obtaining the highest score for that trait.[17] The table shows that, among diplomats, the greatest impact, if all other factors were held constant, obtain for political transcendence, self-esteem, ambition, and hostility, producing shifts ranging from 26% to 61%.[18]

Table 4.2 summarizes the expected impact of selected personality traits on desired war capability, if everything else were held constant. Political transcendence, self-esteem, and trust each have impacts of between .6 and 1.2 war capabilities.[19]

These results, derived simply by substituting values into the derived equations and subtracting to obtain the difference, demonstrate a major result: while R^2 is always small, reflecting the fact that many forces interact to produce a policy, nevertheless the impact of personality traits, everything else being held constant, is very large.

The different patterns of personality engagement are also summarized in Tables 4.1 and 4.2.[20] On most measures the degree of emotional engagement by career diplomats is equal to or greater than that of domestic policy professionals. Clearly there is no good case to be made that norms of rationality within foreign policy elites systematically prevent emotional engagement in their areas of expertise.

The single most striking factor across groups is the higher emotional involvement among military officers. On the predisposition to use force they are more strongly engaged along the hostility and activity-power am-

bition dimension. Their hostility and competitiveness are also more strongly
engaged in their views of what constitutes a desirable war capability. Their
military directness, their tendency to be more emotionally involved in
their decisions and less inhibited by intervening ambiguities, has been
noted by others. As Charles Lerche, writing in the US Army's *Strategic
Subjects Handbook,* put it:

One basic proposition should be made at the outset: there is a generic difference between the way military personnel approach and solve foreign
policy problems and the way their civilian opposite numbers do the same
thing. . . .Probably the most significant characteristic of the military's approach to foreign policy is a strong belief in "can do." There is a great
temptation among orthodox policy makers, when complex and ambiguous
situations are faced, to delay commitment and action until only one
course becomes feasible. . . . To this tendency military spokesmen generally
find themselves opposed; the American military strongly emphasizes the
necessity of solving problems...[21]

Elite Modal Personality and Policy Ambivalence

As the evidence reviewed in chapter 3 demonstrates, these men are not
randomly distributed on these policy-relevant personality traits: there is a
psychological "center of gravity," and thus there are predictable consequences for mutual reinforcement of foreign policy consensus from the
patterns of self-selection, recruitment, and socialization which produce the
modal personality of these American elites.

Several factors *increase* a consensus favorable to American use of force—
especially the personal ambition and competitiveness which characterize
the typical elite respondent. As well, a modest (rather than strong) political liberalism operates in this direction at the State Department, while conservatism moves military officers still further to the hard-line end of the
scale. The high self-esteem among military officers also tends to increase
the confidence with which they support military solutions. Their lower
degree of psychological transcendence—in other words, their relatively
greater tendency to subordinate themselves psychologically to American
foreign policy—would, in comparison with a higher degree of psychological
freedom, increase advocacy of the use of force.

Table 4.1

Impact, Everything Else Held Constant, of Selected Personality Traits on Force Advocacy (Percent)

	OMB	FSO	NWC
1 Hostility	+5	+26	+62
2 Competitiveness (for smaller country scenarios only)	ns	+11	+11
3 Ambition to Feel Active and Powerful	+20	+34	+56
4 Idealization of American Foreign Policy	+97	ns	ns
5 Neurotic Conflict [a]	ns	ns	+27
6 Trust	−16	−16	−16
7 Self-Esteem	−37	−54	+200[b]
8 Political Transcendence	−73	−61	−61
9 Domestic Conservatism[c]	+41	+41	+41

Impact is defined as the difference in the scores on the dependent variable, ceteris paribus, predicted for those obtaining the highest and lowest scores on the trait dimension.

+ or − refers to the direction of impact of an increase of the trait listed.

[a]With *deviations* from overall mean as the dependent variable. In the straightforward test, impact is +9% in all groups.

[b]This figure's magnitude is partly an artifact of small true score variance which makes the regression coefficient take on some of the characteristics of a dummy variable highly collinear with the intercept term—i.e., the estimate is a poor one since there were no truly low self-esteem military officers from which to derive an accurate slope estimate.

[c]Domestic conservatism equation: Percent of cases = 27.36 + 10.9(NWC dummy variable) + 4.06(conservatism score). $p(t)$ for dummy variable $< .02; p(t)$ for conservatism $< 4 \times 10^{-8}, p(F) < 1 \times 10^{-12}, R^2 = .23$, SE = 24.02.

Table 4.2

Impact, Everything Else Held Constant, of Selected Personality Traits on Desired War Capability

	OMB	FSO	NWC
1 Hostility	ns	ns	+.4
2 Competitiveness	ns	ns	+.2
3 Dominance	−.03	ns	ns
4 Trust	−1.3	−.6	−.6
5 Self-Esteem	+1.2	+1.2	−4.9[a]
6 Political Transcendence	−1.1	−1.1	−1.1
7 Domestic Conservatism[b]	+.5	+.5	+.5

Impact is defined as the difference in the scores on the dependent variable, ceteris paribus, predicted for those obtaining the highest and lowest scores on the trait dimension.

+ or − refers to the direction of impact of an increase of the listed trait.

The desired war capability scale range is from ½ to 2½ wars.

[a]This estimate is uncertain due to the absence of low self-esteem military officers—whose presence would allow a more reliable slope estimation—and the resultant presence of a nearly collinear dummy variable in the equation.

[b]Domestic conservatism equation: Capability desired = 1.28 + .049(conservatism score). $p(t)$ and $p(F) < 7 \times 10^{-5}$, $R^2 = .08$, SE = .43.

On the other side, there are several characteristics that work *against*
a consensus in Washington favorable to the use of force. These men tend
to be more friendly than hostile. Of primary importance is the high degree
of trust most have in their fellow men: it is a substantially higher degree of
trust than the average American has for his fellow citizen, and it increases
support for nonmilitary responses to foreign policy problems. Also of importance (given previous research, cited in the notes to chapter 2) is the
relative freedom of these men from major problems of neurotic conflict
(and, at least in the State Department, their low degree of dogmatic rigidity and reflexive authoritarianism). Also decreasing support for military
responses is the high level of self-esteem within the State Department.

This picture of modal tendencies with both reinforcing and conflicting
policy implications suggests that the *typical* FSO, when he advocates or
opposes the use of force, will be *ambivalent,* pulled in opposing directions
within himself. He will experience policy making as *complex.* He will be
unsure of himself, and will feel that each option is to some degree unsatis-
factory. He will rarely experience a complete and bold self-confidence or
peace of mind. However, military officers, with their higher ambition,
higher competitiveness, greater conservatism, and high self-esteem interacting with their professional expertise, will more self-confidently recommend hard-line policies.

Alchemy Versus Science: Foreign Policy as Self-Expression

There is, perhaps, an implicit model in the minds of many people about
how foreign policy is made: policy makers operate as rational scientific
professionals, like engineers. First they specify American national values
and objectives; then they assemble data and evaluate theories about what
effects follow from what causes. Finally they collect relevant data on the
situation at hand, evaluate it, and simply select the best policy.

In practice, of course, there is only a surface resemblance between the
formation of foreign policy (and public policy generally) and what a scientist would accept as a scientific activity. Assuming, for example, that "national security" is one objective, a scientist would propose that a first step
would be to decide clearly what is meant by "national security." Yet there

is major disagreement about even so fundamental a concept; in chapter 3 we saw most military officers tended to think of national security as a matter of capability—of American weapons relative to Russian weapons, and the will to use them. Diplomats tended to think of American security as dependent upon Russian intentions and the quality of the mutual understanding, maturity, and perspective developed in Russian-American relations.

The source of the disagreement is, I think, masked by the fiction that men are talking about some common objective reality when they speak of "security." Rather, security, like much of the objectives in public policy, is a *structure of meaning in the mind of the beholder.*

If scientists disagree about the efficient way to produce a chemical compound, say H_2SO_4, they at least can agree objectively about how that compound looks; but "national security" means different things to different people. Military officers are saying, I think, that they would *personally* feel secure only when America has preponderant strength and destructive potential and the other side knows that it might be used; their personal feelings (private meanings) are displaced onto the topic of "national security." Diplomats tend to feel secure under a different set of circumstances, and their conception of national security reflects a difference in their personal experience of what security means. There is, I suspect, little room for resolving these differences rationally or scientifically because it is only on the surface (i.e., because they use the same words) that these men seem to desire the same external reality.

It is not only with respect to the criteria of national security that men who make foreign policy find themselves in disagreement. This chapter has summarized the evidence that multiple personal predispositions enter into policy preferences. The next chapter analyzes how people implicitly draw upon themselves to create and live within qualitatively different realities.

In a sense these data can be summarized by saying that, regardless of the surface form of the debate, one of the main features of American foreign policy is its exercise as a metaphor for self-expression, "how to be more like me." The mistrustful, competitive, and ambitious men seeking heroic power and excitement think America ought to adopt their style; the cooperative, less ambitious, trusting men think their different approach is to be recommended.

Self-expression in politics can be beneficial, to be sure; perhaps some manifestation of it should be encouraged. It may be that it is one of the generators of values and vision. Self-expression would be entirely appropriate if these men were acting as artists or poets, where it is precisely the personal self-expression of an individual that is valuable. But the problem in foreign policy is that there is an objective reality out there whose structure is independent of the mind and personality of the beholder. You do not turn people loose in a chemical laboratory to mix compounds and chemicals in accordance with their personal styles—not, that is, unless you are completely indifferent to the possibilities that explosions can result from this freedom for self-expressive creativity. Self-expression could be valuable to the art of diplomacy if it were *flexible,* if it were sensitively selected to be effective in reality. Unfortunately, the data in this chapter show that it now operates in a systematic and mechanistic way, even among professionals, always discounting some classes of options in favor of others.

5   Projective Intuition and Emotion-Based Syndromes

In this chapter I will consider the second problem the State Department study was designed to address—the effect of personality traits on the subject's perceptions of other countries. I will then integrate these findings with results from chapter 4 and discuss emotion-based syndromes, specifically their generation of pseudorationality in decision making and the likely importance of a male narcissism syndrome. Next, I will discuss the "best fit" summary equations combining all the data from the State Department study. Finally, I will address several issues raised by FSOs in earlier reactions to these results.

Personality Effects on Perceptions

Chapter 2 established the agenda of testing five traditional theories of how personal characteristics might affect perceptions. For simplicity I will group here as one theory, "self-based inference," the idea (b1) that images of other nations are a straightforward attribution of manifest aspects of personality and the idea (b2) of projection of one's own aspiration to become his ideal self.[1] A second theory (b3), drawn from psychoanalytic observations of ethnocentrism, postulates projection of *repressed* and *submerged* personality characteristics—an inverse self-based inference process. A third theory (b4) is that defects in mental health are the source of misperceptions. A fourth theory (b5) states that men in different groups will, by this fact alone, perceive the world differently. As before, only the statistically significant results are discussed here; details of the analyses will be found in the appendixes.

Self-Based Inference (b1, b2)
Let us consider the perception of Soviet foreign policy.[2] A comparison of scores shows:

l. The more active and powerful a man feels himself to be, the more active and powerful he experiences Soviet foreign policy to be.

2. The more a man desires greater activity and power, the more activity and power he attributes to Soviet foreign policy.

3. The more dominant a man in interpersonal relations, the more activity and power he attributes to Soviet foreign policy.

These results hold in all groups; they show direct self-based inference. In a straightforward way, each man uses himself as an implicit model in constructing a perception of Soviet foreign policy.[3]

It is important to emphasize that, here again, the explanatory power of any one trait in context is quite low; self-based attribution is only part of the story.[4] Nonetheless, these men apparently respond to objective cues that the Soviet Union is active and powerful by drawing on themselves to flesh out a specific image of the degree to which activity and power are dominant.

This interpretation appears especially appropriate when one considers evidence that the same projective effects do *not* appear at all in the case of perceptions of British foreign policy. Britain is not considered aggressive and powerful, and there is much more openness and information about British foreign policy. A man does not *need* to draw upon these aspects of himself to understand the British.[5]

There were also personality effects on the degree of menace experienced from the Soviet Union as recorded on the "friendly-menacing" adjective scale.[6] These results show:

1. The greater a man's tendencies to assert interpersonal dominance the more menace he experiences from the Soviet Union.

2. The more ambitious a man is to feel active and powerful, the more menace he experiences from the Soviet Union.

3. Men who like to compete experience the Soviet Union as more menacing.

Again, these tendencies hold equally across all groups. And, again, there were no comparable effects on the subjects' images of British foreign policy.

If the emphasis on the enhancement of objective cues by self-based inference is correct, then the possibility arises that it may be partly the *secrecy* of Communist foreign policy making that forces these Americans to rely on their imaginations. (If so, then national security secrecy in the

United States would be suspect, because it forces these elites' counterparts in the Soviet Union to rely on *their* imaginations too.)

I will now set forth the evidence from the questionnaire that personal traits significantly affect images of the Soviet Union with regard to a specific situation.

With respect to motives behind Soviet involvement in the Middle East, the following personality traits increase by self-based attribution the probability that a man will see long range, menacing ambition at work, specifically a Soviet desire to sweep across North Africa, take over the Mediterranean, and undermine NATO:[7]

1. How active and powerful a man is at present.[8]

2. How active and powerful a man wishes to feel.[9]

3. The tendency to make long-range plans in one's own life.[10]

Finally, among diplomats, the tendency to make long range plans in the subject's own life increases his belief that the Soviet Union had long range expansionist plans which lay behind its actions in the early cold war years.[11]

Ethnocentrism and Inverse Self-Based Inference (b3)

The theory of projection of repressed aspects of personality (i.e., the attribution to Soviet leaders of the opposite of one's own traits) is not supported by these findings. One final test can be made of the ethnocentrism idea: Does greater idealization of one's group (e.g., of American foreign policy) lead to a more negative image of other nations? The results showed that, on the contrary, there is a positive relation, just a tendency to have either a rosy or pessimistic view of the world.[12,13] Thus we conclude again that these men are not ethnocentric in a way that can be linked to differences in individual psychodynamics.

It should be clear, however, that self-based inference is not always the main story of international politics. For example, the image of the Germans in official propaganda and news coverage during World War II—the image of powerful and lurid evil—was never considered by Americans to be part of their own makeup. The image projected onto the internal viewing screen of the mind's eye in America was probably the "not-self." Thus, while inverse self-based inference probably is true in some situations, it is replaced here by straightforward attribution.

To step back from the data briefly, I would suggest that the partially self-based imaginative processes seen here (compared to inverse self-based imaginative processes at other times) represent an advance toward the achievement of empathy. These men are willing, in some degree, to consider Russian leaders as somewhat like themselves rather than as mysterious, uncivilized monsters. There is a partial effort to "put one's self in the other fellow's shoes" and to try to understand the world as it appears to him, although of course the resulting beliefs may still tell us more about the American than about the Russians.

Mental Health and Perception (b4)

In chapter 4 evidence emerged of the influence of internal psychological conflict on policy. The issue is worth exploring further; the hypothesis that the actions and perceptions a high official adopts are chosen because of clinically ascertainable psychic states, rather than the objective features and constraints of the situations he must deal with, is the basis of a growing number of theories of official behavior. While it is not possible within the limitations of the present study to reach broad conclusions on this issue, we can examine the evidence to see what the influence of ordinary neurotic symptoms might be.

There seems to be little influence on policy attitudes (action) among these men. The only significant findings have been (1) the greater tendency of neurotic military officers to advocate force, and (2) a slight but significant tendency across all groups for higher degrees of neurosis to shift a man more strongly toward the advocacy of force *or* away from it. There has been no discernible effect of neurosis on other foreign policy preferences.

Turning, however, to the effect of neurotic conflicts on perception, it turns out that men who score higher on this scale experience Soviet foreign policy as *less* menacing. And at State and OMB, those with greater intrapsychic conflict tend to be *revisionists*.[14] These results are difficult to understand because of the general nature of the neurotic-symptom scale (e.g., low energy, difficulties in concentration). It may be that such men are engaged in wishful thinking or desire to see a world which does not add to their own existing burdens.[15] But, in truth, the results are a mystery and a subject for future research.

Relative Impacts and (b5) the Organizational Setting

Table 5.1 summarizes the patterns of personality impact across groups. With only one minor difference (which suggests a slightly diminished emotional engagement at OMB), these results show consistent effects across all groups. Organizational setting seems to affect perception less than it affects action.

Again, as in the case of policy advocacy, the evidence is clear that any single personality trait is only one piece of the puzzle. However, each personality trait by itself has a powerful impact if all other influences are held constant.[16] Shifts of up to 42% (4.2 units on a 10-point scale) of how menacing the Soviet Union is experienced to be can be generated by differences in a single personality trait, as can shifts of over 20% in the number of men who believe the Soviet Union has long range expansionist dreams behind its actions in the Middle East.

These results suggest strongly that a combined perception of power and of intention, i.e., of how *menacing* the Soviet Union is, varies more strongly in response to the different personality dynamics of an observer than does the perception of Soviet activity and power alone. They also show that the maximum personality impact is substantially smaller than the range of the scales—a result which tends to support the earlier finding of the cueing of personal emotional engagement in the experience of international reality (i.e., there are broad "ballpark" cues, with personality differences substantially affecting locations within this range).[17]

Elite Modal Personality and Perception

Consistently, across all groups, American elite modal personality (as assessed by typical personality traits of these men) will tend to shape perceptions toward an image of a more powerful, menacing, and expansionist Soviet foreign policy. As we saw in chapter 3, these men experience themselves as

Table 5.1

Impacts, Everything Else Held Constant, of Selected Personality Traits on Perceptions

	OMB	FSO	NWC
I. Soviet Foreign Policy Image			
A. Activity-Power			
Self: Activity-Power	+ 1.6[a]	+ 1.6	+ 1.6
Ideal Self: Activity-Power	+ 2.7	+ 2.7	+ 2.7
Interpersonal Dominance	+ 2.7	+ 2.7	+ 2.7
B. Menace			
Ideal Self: Activity-Power	+ 4.0	+ 4.0	+ 4.0
Interpersonal Dominance	+ 4.2	+ 4.2	+ 4.2
Likes to Compete	+ .8	+ .8	+ .8
Internal Conflict (Neuroticism)	− 2.1	− 2.1	− 2.1
II. Soviet Expansionist Ambitions in Middle East			
Self: Activity-Power	+19.3[b]	+19.3	+19.3
Ideal Self: Activity-Power	+21.5	+21.5	+21.5
Life Planning: Long Range Goal Orientation	+13.9	+13.9	+13.9
III. Soviet Ambitious Goals Responsible for Cold War (Orthodox view)			
Life Planning: Long Range Goal Orientation	0	+11.7	na
Internal Conflict (Neuroticism)	−14.1	−14.1	na

na = not available.

[a]Entries for part I of table are given as positions on 10-point scale.

[b]Entries for parts II, III are given as percent shifts.

active and powerful, and wish to feel still more active and powerful, they
are slightly more dominant than submissive, many like to compete, substantial numbers make long range career plans, and they are relatively free
of neurotic symptoms.[18] (On most of these traits military officers score so
as to find intuitively more plausible, thus to experience with more confidence, a more menacing image of the Soviet Union.) It seems possible that
some of these same modal traits could characterize Soviet foreign policy
elites and shape similar Soviet beliefs about American policy and intentions.

Summary of Personality Effects on Perception
There is a certain dreamlike quality involved in the behavioral and perceptual dynamics sketched in the foregoing sections. A man experiences other
nations *internally,* in his own mind; they are creations which partly embody
his own emotions. In part, the men studied here frighten or reassure themselves by working their own oppressive or domineering or menacing or in-
trusive predispositions into their experiences of the Soviet Union. Like the
god Vishnu, these men partly dream the world in which they act and in
which, as a consequence of foreign policy decisions, we all live.

It is true, of course, that diplomats think, analyze, and test out their
thinking against what facts they have. I think they *try* to be rational. But
in making choices based upon incomplete knowledge, and having of necessity to deal with ambiguous situations, and to use crude, inadequately
validated theories of political behavior, they resort to projective intuition.
And that resort systematically shapes the mental simulation these men
construct of the world without complete grounding in objective evidence.
The use of these processes tends to trap a man by his own character structure and emotional dynamics.

Emotion-Based Syndromes of Action and Cognition

The Psychology of Self-Deception
The most striking perspective on the findings in chapter 4 and in this
chapter is that personality traits shape both (1) policy preferences and
(2) perceptions of the intentions of other nations simultaneously *and in*

directions which tend to yield internal coherence between action and cognition. The result is what *looks* like a rational decision, and *feels* like a rational decision, but which is in reality only a plausible, consistent decision.[19] For example an ambitious, competitive man is inclined to use force *and* he is also inclined by the same personality traits to imagine opponents with expansionist ambitions against whom hard-line policies are called for (see, e.g., President Kennedy's decision at the Bay of Pigs discussed in chapter 1).[20] Similarly, unambitious, cooperative men tend to oppose the use of force and are also predisposed by the same personality traits to see relatively unambitious, quiescent, friendly nations against whom hard-line policies are not appropriate.

Foreign policy decision makers regularly say they have made the most rational choices possible. The evidence clarifies how they come genuinely to feel this way—and how they are led to deceive themselves. Internally consistent and plausible decisions do not necessarily have a rational base, and journalists and scholars will mislead people if they mistake rationalizations for true explanations.

Male Narcissism Syndromes

I want to draw to the reader's attention corroborating evidence from other disciplines that some males do evidence emotion-based, self-deceptive syndromes such as those detailed here. The results of anthropological studies have now become readily available in standard computer format, and this has allowed anthropologists to analyze the relation between characteristics of tribes and their war propensity. Recently published analyses of these data from over 100 primitive societies show that one predictor of war, among others, is the tendency of males in a society to be ambitious and competitive—the same correlation between personality traits and war found in the State Department study.[21]

Several of these investigators have explored the subject further and have concluded that male sexual dynamics are implicated in this connection, and specifically that there is indeed an emotion-based "machismo" or male narcissism syndrome in some tribes which includes not only personality and action linkages but also personality and perception linkages of a paranoid nature (e.g., feelings of insecurity, suspiciousness, the tendency to be easily enraged by imagined threats). It is interesting to note that the

political scientist Nathan Leites published a psychoanalytic study of Russian leaders 25 years ago and concluded that they exhibited a similar syndrome.[22]

As of this writing the problem of narcissism syndromes is also an area
of rapid theoretical growth in American psychoanalysis, and there are continuing debates about internal mechanisms and conceptual vocabulary. It
is not clear whether male narcissism syndromes are directly an expression
of sexual dynamics or whether these are peripheral to "structural" problems (e.g., a split of a man's sense of himself so he feels both grandiose *and*
inferior.) It would be digressive to review all of these technical issues here.
I want simply to note that there is growing attention and agreement about
such syndromes from widely diverse sources—including the broad-based investigations of anthropologists. And most of these writers agree that there
is an emotion-based syndrome, similar to that in the State Department
study, linking ambition, aggressiveness, and paranoid tendencies. However,
such a machismo syndrome is attentuated in the State Department in com-
parision with the overt arrogance, grandiosity, sadism, and terror which
characterize males in some primitive tribes which social scientists have
studied. And while several women in the State Department felt that a
strong male chauvinist attitude (another correlate of the syndrome) was
present there, this too is probably attenuated in comparison to that of
some primitive tribes.

It is important to emphasize, at the same time, that machismo has
many facets. To be strong, proud, powerful, hard, tough, particularly sensitive and alert to possible threats or domination by others, to be boldly
assertive, are some of these. But male chauvinism also has connotations of
paternalism, of providing security and valued gratifications, of being a
protector, a leader, guardian, benefactor, a provider. Machismo in the
State Department could include the virtues of paternalism (at least as
these are seen by the paternalist). To put it candidly, I suspect at least
some of these men wish to be high status managers, leaders, and benefactors to the world—and they are willing to fight stubbornly rather than
surrender America's chance to play this powerful role of active virility,
guidance of others, self-worth, and generativity.

That international politics is a "world of men" is a central and probably consequential fact; one that may illuminate underlying sexual dynamics, and one that is important to the extent that males are more inclined than women to seek strength, power, activity, dominance, competitive achievment (and there is a large body of literature that this is the case in America):[23] such qualities make them more fearful of others and more predisposed to unleash violence (perhaps especially against ungrateful small countries).[24]

I do not intend to single out the State Department as unique in having ambitious males with the desire to be high status benefactors of others. The available evidence suggests such dreams may be widespread among males in American society.[25] And perhaps becoming a member of a political elite is attractive to ambitious men in many countries.

Best Prediction Equations

As we saw in chapter 3, many of the variables pertinent to this study overlap (i.e., correlate with) each other. Since some readers will be interested in the most parsimonious mathematical statement of my findings, I present in tables 5.2–5.5 the results of the cumulative explanatory power of the perceptual and personality variables in the study when overlaps are controlled.

The first characteristic of the equations is the independent impact of a man's beliefs about "who started the cold war?" For both the tendency to use force (table 5.2) and desired war capability levels (table 5.3) this fundamental belief is of marked importance, more important than the (nonsignificant) effects of images of *current* Soviet foreign policy.

We can make sense of this, I think, by linking this finding with the analysis of international-relations games in the laboratory. Terhune found that *first round* experiences tend to be of critical importance.[26] For example, perceived treachery in a first round tended to form a basic interpretive framework or gestalt which shaped later mistrustful behavior. Men lived in history and did not continually recompute their fundamental assumptions about the true nature of the world. It seems, then, that the continuing argument about the origins of the cold war is more than an arcane academic debate. If the revisionists win, then interpretations and responses to Soviet foreign policy now, thirty years later, will also shift significantly.

Table 5.2

Best Prediction Equation, Tendency to Advocate Use of Force (Percent)

a_o	b		$p(t)$
22.35	3.526 (1.527)	Interaction of ideal self: Activity-power and self-esteem	.03
	1.416 (.664)	NWC—Interaction of ideal self: Activity-power and self-esteem	.04
	2.900 (.772)	Domestic conservatism	3×10^{-4}
	1.724 (.799)	Relative Soviet responsibility for origins of cold war	.04
	− .995 (.492)	Interpersonal trust	.05
	− 3.493 (2.259)	Political transcendence	.13

$R^2 = .31$ $F(6,196) = 14.66$

SE = 22.97 $p(F) < 1 \times 10^{-13}$

The number in parenthesis beneath each b coefficient is the standard error of that coefficient. Dividing a b coefficient by its standard error gives the value of a t statistic, which in turn yields the probability $p(t)$, listed in the right-hand column, that the value of b might have resulted from random processes.

Table 5.3

Best Prediction Equation, Desired General Military Capability (Number of Wars)

a_0	b		$p(t)$
0.84	.061 (.014)	Relative degree of Soviet responsibility for cold war	3×10^{-5}
	.032 (.012)	Domestic conservatism	.009

$R^2 = .16$ $F(2,187) = 17.75$
$SE = .414$ $p(F) < 9 \times 10^{-8}$

Table 5.4

Best Prediction Equation, Soviet Foreign Policy: Activity-Power

a_0	b		$p(t)$
5.28	.236 (.077)	Interaction of ideal self: Activity-power and self-esteem	.003
	.072 (.034)	Domestic conservatism	.05

$R^2 = .11$ $F(2,220) = 7.6$
$SE = .96$ $p(F) < 7 \times 10^{-4}$

Table 5.5

Best Prediction Equation, Soviet Foreign Policy Attributed Menace

a_0	b		$p(t)$
4.43	−.21 (.07)	Neuroticism	.004
	.402 (.190)	Ideal self: Activity-power	.04

$R^2 = .10$ $F(2,218) = 6.94$
$SE = 2.13$ $p(F) < .002$

The evidence is that the revisionists have been gaining ground: although few diplomats have shifted across the dividing line to the revisionist side, the younger a diplomat, the less completely traditional are his views.[27] This is the primary route through which age has a systematic influence on foreign policy.

The second characteristic of the tables is that an interaction term, the tendency to wish to feel active and powerful and *simultaneously* to be of high self-esteem, is central in increasing the use of force and the belief that Soviet foreign policy is active and powerful.

Finally, the tables show that domestic conservatism or liberalism is a strong predictor when used in equations with other relevant personality variables and perceptions. [28]

The independent impacts of these variables, when all are considered together and their overlaps controlled, can be assessed easily by multiplying the b coefficients by 10 (since all variables have been rescaled from 0 to 10). The R^2 statistics are respectable in showing personality-based themes underlying and shaping complex thought processes, and R^2 is .31 in the case of the use of force.

These results also help to clarify whether the organizational setting exercises an independent effect on either policy or perception. The evidence from chapter 3 showed such information was a useful *descriptive* rule-of-thumb for identifying differences. But the organizational setting itself is not usually a significant predictor of the perceptions and policy decisions studied here which adds causal information once the personality traits are known.

Reactions and Criticisms

Each participant who requested it (almost all did so) received a detailed summary of the data and the conclusions drawn from them. About 5% of FSOs communicated reactions, and comments were also solicited from several psychiatrists and social scientists familiar with the State Department. All those who offered reactions agreed that the results plausibly agreed with their own observations of foreign policy thinking. But several comments raised important and useful clarifications of what the State

Department study accomplished and what it implies and does not imply. These clarifications are discussed in the remainder of this chapter.

In a sense the findings are reassuring.
This observation was advanced on the basis of the statistics which show that any single personality trait plays only a small part within the over-all context and that, taken together, the personality traits studied explain only about 31% of the variance in the advocacy of force—and this in scenarios which are in fact unrepresentative of situations usually encountered. Hence, one writer concluded, irrationality plays a minor role in American foreign policy.

I disagree with this conclusion. It must be recognized that this was far from an exhaustive study—it consisted of assessing those personality traits which could be fitted into a 45-minute questionnaire. There are many additional facets of personality which may be relevant. Furthermore, the scales were generally short, hence the scores somewhat more randomly variable (and correlations thus probably lower) than longer scales would have produced. What can be said is that the 31% figure represents a *minimum* estimate, a floor. It may be that the true percentage of variations in the advocacy of force explained by personality factors could be higher, possibly much higher. No one will know without further research. And even the 31% figure indicates that, unless some other factors are of overwhelming importance in a particular case, the personality of the decision maker can be of crucial importance in tilting a decision one way or another.

Also, it is scarcely true that personality-based irrationality is the only source of irrationality. As reviewed briefly in chapter 2, stress and group pressures toward "groupthink" are two other sources of an emotional nature. As well, biased cognitive processes—drawing inappropriate historical analogies, for example—can also undermine foreign policy rationality; and "operational codes" or rules of thumb inappropriate to a particular situation may produce ineffective or disastrous policies. There is no warrant for concluding that irrationality has been dealt with by this study in any other than one of its aspects.

Finally, I agree that the materials presented to the subjects, centered as they were on plausible scenarios for the use of force, are unrepresentative of the everyday issues in foreign policy. Considering *all* of the situations confronting American decision makers, the question of the advocacy of military force seldom arises. And one may not need to give a significant role to personality to understand much of this routine diplomacy. But there has been no claim to construct or test a total theory of international relations or of American foreign policy. What *is* at issue are those infrequent but disproportionately consequential cases where the use of military force becomes a real possibility. And in these cases personality-based thinking can play a substantial role.

The study is biased toward casting aspersions on those who take hard-line positions.
It is not my intention to single out any one policy position as irrational. In fact, the data do not support such a conclusion: there is a lock-in effect of personality dynamics on thought across the entire spectrum, and personality-based thinking is just as characteristic of doves as of hawks and of those in between.

Nevertheless, it is true that my central concern has been that force can be used too quickly and unrealistically: the Bay of Pigs is an example of such a case; Vietnam is another. Both were events in my own lifetime that helped convince me there was a problem here to be explored. And Deutsch's review of the evidence (discussed in chapter 1) that the majority of those governments initiating official violence in the twentieth century have lost does suggest that overreliance on such policies is a typical error of nations in the twentieth century. But it would be a mistake to conclude (as my critic felt some readers might conclude) that, for example, détente is established here as a more rational policy toward the Soviet Union, and that its hard line critics are more irrational.

Don't we know this already?
The answer to the question, "Don't we know this already?" is "Yes—and no." There probably are many people who have sensed, both in themselves and from their observations of public events, that major policy decisions

are personalized, the final choice a self-expression of the decision maker himself. It is the mark of good social science research that it clarifies and explicates experience, that people will, upon reflection, say "of course."

But, if perhaps sensed, it is doubtful that the precise mechanisms of the influence of personality have heretofore been explicitly perceived. I found in talking with men at the State Department that a personality-based explanation of why men disagreed was not a *readily available* one, especially in a man's understanding of himself. This recognition may have been *latent,* but it was not easily accessible as a perspective on the process in which these men were engaged. And chapter 2 reviewed a variety of competing ideas among specialists, both about causation in international relations and about the form personality-based influence might take. Without data, no one knew what the actual story would be: some scholars have maintained personality influences to be trivial (except in cases of marked pathology, e.g., Hitler); other writers have contended that they might be significant for virtually every decision maker. But no one has previously explicitly proposed that features of American elite modal personality increase the predisposition to war, and, with evidence acquired directly and by explicit methods, that major foreign policy decision making must be conceived *generally* as in part an unreliable resort to self-expression and systematic projective intuition to deal with and make sense out of an ambiguous world. In this way the answer is "no," we did not know this already.

There is, however, an important issue left unanswered by the State Department study: FSOs or military officers do not make foreign policy. Politicians make it, and they make it through a process of consultation, analysis, and debate. Are the same dynamics found in the State Department study actually causative in real world policy making? The following chapter takes up this problem directly.

6   Personality and American Foreign Policy, 1898–1968

The State Department study provides evidence for systematic effects of emotional dynamics on both action and perception. But those results were obtained from a study of the 229 mid-level subjects who answered the questionnaire in early 1972. Do such dynamics also color or even in some cases determine the formulation of actual foreign policy decisions made by heads of state? One could argue they might not: the American government spends billions of dollars for a process of *collective* rational analysis. If the process works well, then one might expect individual predispositions unsupported by objective analysis to vanish when exposed to searching criticism.

But one can be skeptical of this; for major issues of American foreign policy, the president must eventually apply his own judgment to situations that often are ambiguous and uncertain. A recent comparative study supports the presumption that the personality of the president can be crucial. Donley and Winter scored American presidential inaugural speeches from T. Roosevelt to Nixon for achievement and power motivation.[1] They correlated these measures with whether or not a war occurred during the later years the president was in office, and they report a significant ($p < .15$) .40 partial point biserial correlation between presidential power motivation and subsequent war.

The Donley-Winter study is supporting evidence, but it can be interpreted in many ways. Since the assessment of personality was based on a single document rather than on a study of actual behavior across time, it is not the best conceivable measure. And motive scores in Inaugural Addresses may, for example, also reflect a mood of the country in addition to the personality of the president.[2]

The State Department study, the Donley-Winter investigation, the cross-cultural anthropological studies, and Eckhardt's summary of the private dimensions of ideology[3] converge to suggest that central personality predispositions generalized by self-expression in foreign policy choices involving force are dominance-seeking, ambitious, self-assertive traits. The historical study to be described in this chapter was designed to assess whether there is evidence for such personality effects on actual foreign policy decisions made by presidents between 1898 and 1968.

I intend to proceed quite carefully in this study. The attention to method, especially the concerns with reliability of measures, sampling, and the ruling out of alternative explanations, may seem tedious to some readers, but I think this care is justified because it matters a great deal whether the theories tested here are right, whether they are more solidly grounded than plausible speculation.

The Design of the Study, and Personality Ratings

It should be clear that the question posed for test is not whether "personality" influences policy. Broadly construed, "personality" refers to many characteristics of decision makers (e.g., intelligence, cultural values, and identification with the welfare of their nation) that probably are always relevant. But such constant *shared* characteristics can either be assumed or subsumed under higher levels of analysis. The theoretical question addressed here is whether intra-elite *variations* in personality characteristics produce *variations* in policy preference so that some personality characteristics unique to a key decision maker need to be measured and taken into account to explain why some policies are adopted rather than others.

It should also be clear that what is being tested is not a general theory of foreign-policy-making behavior—there is no claim that "personality traits produce wars" alone. Rather the question is whether certain personality traits have, in certain situations, actually tipped the balance for or against a policy choice like war.

The research method employed in this study was to work backward, to select cases of American intra-elite policy disagreements and then to test the proposition that the direction of such disagreements could be consistently predicted from independently derived knowledge of personality differences between the participants.[4] If personality differences show only a random correlation with the direction of policy disagreement, then it cannot be said that such personality differences produced policy differences. But if the imaginary random control group of the null hypothesis is rejected, then the conclusion would be that, in the confirming cases, the observed personality difference was probably the crucial contributor to the actual policy outcome.

It should be noted that interpersonal generalization theory would also predict that policy *agreement* should tend to flow from *similar* personality traits. This is a second test which could have been conducted. I do not, however, believe it would have been as straightforward and direct a test. Presidents tend to favor as secretaries of state and key advisers men who share their own views, and there is thus implicit pressure for them to agree to retain influence. My assumption was that such situational and other pressures toward "groupthink" will often confound or override personality similarity as a factor in producing agreement.[5] Agreement will tend to be broken, I assumed, only by strongly felt (hence probably personality based) differences. In other words, I expected less confounding of other factors in producing disagreement, and I selected the present design as a better (albeit more limited) test to give personality factors a direct chance to register their impact.

By focusing on intra-elite disagreements at the same point in time, major alternative hypotheses are held constant. The domestic and international situations are the same for all participants. (The major competing hypothesis not explicitly ruled out by this design is the possibility that intra-elite roles are a significant influence—e.g., that a secretary of state would tend to oppose military options by virtue of his office. If personality differences and policy differences correlate separately with office, then a correlation between the first two may not be a causal relationship. I will return to this problem later.)

Thirty-six men were selected for study—American presidents, secretaries of state, and selected advisers who served between 1898 and 1968 (table 6.1). Personality traits were assessed by searching scholarly works, insiders' accounts, biographies, and autobiographies for the men under consideration. Passages relevant to two personality dimensions—general *dominance over subordinates* and *extraversion* were excerpted by me, retyped (omitting explicit clues that would identify the individual involved or the scholarly source), and included in dossiers. These dossiers were rated (in random order) using the criteria reported in the notes of tables 6.2 and 6.3 by two independent judges who did not know the identities of the men they rated. I, who knew the identities and the scholarly sources, also rated the men. Among the three judges correlations ranged from .83 to .91 ($p < .001$) for dominance, and between .84 and .93 for extraversion ($p < .001$). There

Table 6.1

Comparative Personality Assessments: Presidents, Secretaries of State, and Selected Advisers, 1898–1968

	Introvert			Extravert
High Dominance	Dulles			Johnson
	Wilson			Roosevelt, F.
				Roosevelt, T.
	Hoover	Acheson	Byrnes	
	Hughes	House	Hopkins	
	Stimson	Hull	Kennedy	
		Root		
	Herter	Colby	Bacon	Bryan
	Kennan	Knox	McKinley	Taft
	Marshall	Lansing	Stettinius	
			Stevenson	
			Truman	
Low Dominance	Coolidge	Kellogg	Eisenhower	Harding
	Day	Rusk	Hay	
	Sherman			

Intervals between categories are shown as equal here for display only; they should not be taken as equal in fact. Hypotheses were tested with numerical scores.

were no systematic differences among us, and the unweighted mean rating
of the three judges was used as a subject's rating on that personality dimension—except in the case of William Jennings Bryan. Knowing the original sources of the ratings for Bryan, I felt that it was the less scholarly
and more idealized accounts that gave him a high dominance rating; I low-
ered his dominance score, since I felt the lower score would be more accurate.

The task of second hand personality assessment of historical figures
presents troublesome methodological issues. In the first instance, a man's
observed behavior can differ substantially depending upon his role and his
relation with those with whom he is interacting. A man like Secretary
Dulles could be dominant over his subordinates yet deferential to a superior.
This social context must be explicitly taken into account, and treated in a
standardized manner. I chose to assess dominance over nominal subordinates, on the assumption that a man's desire to dominate would be less inhibited and show itself more clearly in this sector of his life. In addition,
since America's use of force has often been against small countries, I felt
this was the most relevant tendency of interpersonal behavior that would
generalize.[6] Special weight was given to the scope and level of activity
through which these men sought to initiate, monitor, and give personal
direction to the activities of their subordinates. Thus an individual was
described as very high on dominance if he was "recorded as regularly intervening at lower levels *or* ignoring subordinates completely *while setting
policy himself.* May berate subordinates, seeks to impose will forcefully.
He runs the show. Complex variegated information acquistion system." A
very low dominance individual was one who "seldom interferes, defers to
others, almost welcomes initiatives of others as a relief. Doesn't as much
share power as abdicate it."

Criteria to assess extraversion were specifically constructed to take into
account situational differences between men in these offices and a more representative sample of the population. Most of these men, by virtue of
their public offices, probably spent more time with more people than
the average American. They probably had more friends and acquaintances.
Accordingly, to differentiate among them, special weight was given to how
a man spent what little leisure time he had: did he spend it with large

Table 6.2

An Inventory of Policy Disagreements: Coercion and Threat (Hypothesis 1)

Subjects	Description
1 T. Roosevelt vs. McKinley	Roosevelt was an earlier advocate of the Spanish-American War.[a]
2 T. Roosevelt vs. Hay	Roosevelt objected to the first Hay-Pauncefote Treaty because he wanted the Isthmian canal fortified.
3 T. Roosevelt vs. Hay	Against Hay's objection Roosevelt used veiled threats in the Alaskan boundary arbitration with England.
4 T. Roosevelt vs. Root, Bacon	Root and Bacon opposed sending American troops to Cuba in 1906.
5 T. Roosevelt vs. Root	Roosevelt was very reluctant to agree to 24 bilateral arbitration treaties negotiated by Root.
6 T. Roosevelt vs. Root	Root opposed Roosevelt's desire to intervene mililarily in Venezuela.
7 Knox vs. Root	While in private life Root dissented from a Knox ultimatum to Chile.
8 Wilson vs. Root, Taft, Bryan, Bacon	Root, Taft, Bryan, and Bacon opposed Wilson's military intervention in Mexico. (Bryan acquiesced until the Vera Cruz landing).
9 T. Roosevelt vs. Wilson, Root, Taft, Bryan, Bacon	Roosevelt wanted Wilson's Mexican policy to be more forceful.
10 T. Roosevelt, Lansing vs. Wilson	Roosevelt and Lansing wanted earlier American entry into World War I.

References	Number Consistent with Hypothesis	Number Not Consistent with Hypothesis
Howard K. Beale, *Theodore Roosevelt and the Rise of America to World Power* (Baltimore: Johns Hopkins University Press, 1956) pp. 61–63 et passim.	1	0
William Thayer, *The Life and Letters of John Hay,* vol. 2 (Boston: Houghton Mifflin, 1915), pp. 339–341.	1	0
Foster Rhea Dulles, "John Hay" in Norman A. Graebner (ed.), *An Uncertain Tradition: American Secretaries of State in the Twentieth Century* (New York: McGraw Hill, 1961), pp. 22–39, esp. p. 36.	1	0
Philip C. Jessup, *Elihu Root,* vol. 2 (New York: Dodd, Mead, 1938), p. 156; James B. Scott, "Robert Bacon" in S. F. Bemis (ed.), *The American Secretaries of State and Their Diplomacy,* vol. 9 (New York: Cooper Square, 1963), p. 290.	2	0
Charles Toth, "Elihu Root" in Graebner (ed.) (see entry 3), pp. 40–58, p. 56.	1	0
Ibid., p. 48.	1	0
Jessup (entry 4), vol. 2, p. 250.	0	1
Ibid., pp. 259–61, 256; Richard Challener, "William Jennings Bryan" in Graebner (ed.) (entry 3), pp. 79–100, p. 92; Merle Curti, "Bryan and World Peace," *Smith College Studies in History,* vol. 16, no. 3–4 (April–July, 1931), pp. 180–181; James B. Scott, *Robert Bacon: Life and Letters* (New York: Doubleday, Page, 1923), p. 265.	4	0
W. H. Harbough, *The Life and Times of Theodore Roosevelt,* rev. ed. (New York: Collier, 1963), p. 450. Also see references for entry 8.	4	1 Roosevelt-Wilson, no difference
Jessup (entry 4), pp. 321–323, et passim.	0	2

Table 6.2 (continued)

Subjects	Description
11 T. Roosevelt, Wilson, Lansing vs. Root	Root opposed Wilson's "path to war" policies prior to the sinking of the *Lusitania.*
12 T. Roosevelt, Wilson, House, Root, Lansing vs. Bryan	Bryan resigned as Secretary of State in opposition to Wilson's movements toward entering World War I.
13 Hughes vs. Harding	Harding dissented from a stiff stand against the Obregon government of Mexico urged by Hughes in a dispute over American property claims.
14 Hughes vs. Harding	Hughes wanted to keep US forces in Haiti in 1923; Harding wanted to withdraw them.
15 Hoover vs. Stimson	Hoover opposed Stimson's desire to "put teeth" into the Kellogg-Briand pact by invoking economic sanctions against Japanese aggression in Manchuria.
16 Hoover vs. Stimson	Hoover was a stronger advocate of disarmament than Stimson.
17 Acheson, Dulles vs. Kennan	Kennan advocated halting the northern advance of Allied forces in Korea at the 38th parallel.
18 Acheson, Dulles, vs. Kennan	Kennan dissented strongly from the militarization of containment urged by both men.[b]
19 Dulles vs. Eisenhower	Eisenhower opposed the Dulles plan for the US to intervene in Indochina to rescue and supplant the French.[c]
20 Dulles vs. Acheson	Acheson opposed the Dulles policy of a strong military stand to retain Quemoy and Matsu.
21 Dulles vs. Acheson	In the 1958–1959 Berlin deadline crisis Acheson felt the Dulles policy was too conciliatory.
22 Kennedy vs. Rusk, Stevenson	Rusk had misgivings about, and Stevenson wholly disapproved of, the Bay of Pigs invasion.
23 Acheson vs. Kennedy, Stevenson	Acheson favored a more hard-line stance than Kennedy or Stevenson in the 1961 Berlin crisis.
24 Kennedy vs. Stevenson	During the same crisis Stevenson urged a more conciliatory stand than Kennedy selected.

References	Number Consistent with Hypothesis	Number Not Consistent with Hypothesis
Ibid., pp. 321–333.	2	1
Challener (entry 8), p. 98.	5	0
Robert K. Murray, *The Harding Era,* (Minneapolis: University of Minnesota Press, 1969), pp. 329–331.	1	0
Ibid., p. 334.	1	0
Elting Morison, *Turmoil and Tradition: A Study of the Life and Times of Henry L. Stimson* (Boston: Houghton Mifflin, 1960), pp. 382–383, 403–405, 445.	0	1
Ibid., p. 410.	0	1
George F. Kennan, *Memoirs, 1925–1950* (New York: Bantam, 1969), p. 523.	2	0
Ibid., pp. 497–528 et passim; idem. *Memoirs, 1950–1963* (Boston: Little, Brown, 1972) passim.	2	0
Hans J. Morgenthau, "John Foster Dulles" in Graebner (ed.) (entry 3), pp. 289–308, p. 296.	1	0
New York Times, Sept. 7, 1958, p. 1.	1	0
New York Times, Nov. 19, 1959, pp. 1, 12.	0	1
Edward Weintal and Charles Bartlett, *Facing the Brink* (New York: Scribner, 1967), p. 149; Arthur M. Schlesinger, Jr., *A Thousand Days* (Boston: Houghton Mifflin, 1965), pp. 259, 271.	2	0
Schlesinger (entry 22), pp. 380–383.	1	1
Ibid., 346.	1	0

Table 6.2 (continued)

Subjects	Description
25 Acheson vs. Kennedy, Stevenson	Acheson consistently favored the air strike option during the Cuban missile crisis.
26 Kennedy vs. Stevenson	Stevenson favored negotiations during the missile crisis; Kennedy adopted a quarantine.
27 Kennedy, Johnson vs. Kennan	Kennan dissented from Kennedy and Johnson policies in Vietnam.
28 Johnson vs. Kennan	During the Soviet invasion of Czechoslovakia Kennan advocated sending 100,000 American troops to Europe; Johnson did not agree.

I chose to consider disagreements arising between men who *advocated* different positions. Men who tended to "go along" with the policy initiatives of others were usually excluded. For example, in entry 2, I counted only the Roosevelt-Hay disagreement (rather than including the Roosevelt-McKinley comparison which would also have been supportive of interpersonal generalization theory) because McKinley tended to take a back seat in foreign policy formation. The Roosevelt-McKinley comparison is included, however, on the issues surrounding the Spanish-American War because McKinley did become actively involved at that time. The reader should be cautioned that this early decision was a matter of some consequence since the men who tend to "go along" turn out to be lower on interpersonal dominance. In other words, the high percentages reported favorably for interpersonal generalization theory are somewhat sensitive to this decision.

I have, after considerable uncertainty, excluded comparisons between Colonel House and Woodrow Wilson on American entry into World War I and between Harry Hopkins and Franklin Roosevelt on American entry into World War II. Both advisers appeared, at times, to be more inclined to advocate military involvement at an earlier point than the president. However, both Wilson and Roosevelt were sensitive to public opinion, and it is a reasonable interpretation of their behavior that they did not move until after a buildup of public opinion; thus, I am not sure that their "true" opinions (the attitudes they would urge on a president if they were his adviser) actually differed from the views House or Hopkins may have been freer to express. The matter need not be resolved here; but it should be noted that including these two cases would slightly increase the number of cases inconsistent with interpersonal generalization theory.

It should also be noted that the cases listed here predominantly involve American

References	Number Consistent with Hypothesis	Number Not Consistent with Hypothesis
Graham T. Allison, *Essence of Decision: Explaining the Cuban Missile Crisis* (Boston: Little, Brown, 1971), p. 208 et passim.	1	1
Schlesinger (entry 22), pp. 807–808.	1	0
J. William Fulbright (ed.), *The Vietnam Hearings* (New York: Random House, 1966), pp. 107–166.	2	0
New York Times, September 22, 1968, p. 3.	0	1
Totals	38	11
Percentages	77.5%	22.5%
Probability[d]	$p < .0001$	

use of force in smaller-country arenas. Great-power wars may involve such weighty and costly decisions as to overwhelm the personal motive differences discussed here for those who feel under attack.

Were Bryan's dominance score the original 5.67 instead of my adjusted value of 3.67 there would be a change of 2 cases (the Root (5.33) and Lansing (4.00) comparisons in item 12) in the inconsistent column leaving 36 supportive cases and 13 opposed (73.4% supportive).

The question has also arisen whether including men out of office biases these scores. Looking at the subset of only those holding formal offices, we would lose 25 comparisons of which 17 are consistent with hypotheses 1 (1 each for items 2, 17, 20, 23, and 25; 2 from cases 8, 11, 12, and 27; 4 from case 9) and 8 inconsistent (1 each from items 7, 9, 10, 11, 21, 23, 25, and 28). This leaves 24 cases of which 21 support, hypothesis 1—an increase of confimation to 87.5% of the 24 cases ($p < .0001$).

Mean dominance scores (extraversion scores in parentheses) used to test hypotheses were Johnson, 9.67 (9.00); Dulles, 9.33 (1.33); Franklin Roosevelt, 9.33 (9.67); Wilson, 8.67 (2.33); Roosevelt, 8.67, (8.33); Hoover, 8.33 (1.33); House, 8.33 (4.33); Hughes, 8.00 (2.00); Stimson, 7.67 (2.33); Kennedy, 6.67 (6.33); Hopkins, 6.00 (6.67); Brynes, 6.00 (6.33); Hull, 5.33 (4.87); Acheson, 5.33 (4.00); Root, 5.33 (4.33); Lansing, 4.00 (4.13); Bryan, 3.67 (adjusted from 5.67) (7.67); Stevenson, 3.67 (6.33); Stettinius, 3.67 (6.33); Knox, 3.67 (4.00); Bacon, 3.67 (6.33); Truman, 3.67 (7.33); Colby, 3.67 (4.00); Marshall, 3.33 (2.33); Herter, 3.33 (2.67); Taft, 3.33 (7.67); Kennan, 3.00 (2.00); McKinley, 3.00 (2.00); Kellogg, 2.67 (3.00); Eisenhower, 2.33 (5.00); Rusk, 2.33 (3.00); Hay, 1.67 (6.00); Sherman, 1.67 (2.00); Day, 1.67 (2.00); Harding, 1.67 (8.67); Coolidge, 1.33 (1.67).

Scoring criteria for dominance were (1–10)—*Highest scoring:* Recorded as regu-

Table 6.2 (continued)

larly intervening at lower levels *or* ignoring subordinates completely *while setting policy himself.* May berate subordinates, seeks to impose will forcefully. He runs the show. Complex, variegated information acquisition system. *Mod High:* In command of situation, may bypass channels. Some power sharing and flexibility. *Mod:* Sets guidelines and makes final decisions himself. Fair amount of autonomy to subordinates. Tends to work through channels. *Mod Low:* Often takes a stand, primarily to check excesses. Generally grants large amount of autonomy to subordinates. Appoints men and tends to stay out of their way. *Low:* Seldom interferes, defers to others, almost welcomes initiatives of others as a relief. Doesn't as much share power as abdicate it.

Scoring criteria for Introversion-Extraversion were (1–10)—*High Ext.:* Emotionally out-going, loves crowds. Enjoys contacts with many kinds of people. Leisure time spent with people. *Mod. High:* Warm, out-going, affable, possibly not drawn to crowds. Likes to socialize in his leisure time. *Mod:* Mixed—usually warm and considerate, especially with a moderate number of friends, sometimes seen as a bit withdrawn. *Mod Low:* Reticent, shy, self-controlled, unemotional, leisure time in relative isolation, *Low:* Cold, icy, or aloof, or acutely shy. Few or no close friends, leisure time spent away from people.

[a] While I have followed the weight of scholarly opinion in scoring McKinley as opposed to the Spanish-American War and being pressured into it, this view is not universal. See, for example, Walter LaFeber, *The New Empire: An Interpretation of American Expansion 1860–1898* (Ithaca: Cornell University Press, 1963).

[b] This case could include Kennan's dissent from the Truman Doctrine in the early cold war period (he felt it too sweeping). See George F. Kennan, "American Involvement" in Marcus G. Raskin and Bernard B. Fall (eds.), *The Viet-Nam Reader* (New York: Vintage, 1967). revised ed., pp. 15–31, pp. 17–18. The origin of containment is not explained, on the American side, by personality traits revealed by the personality differences model. But the sweeping implementation, military emphasis, and structuring of the cold war do seem to be shaped by personality traits.

[c] I have followed the weight of scholarly opinion concerning Dulles' thinking. For a different view consult Robert Randle, *Geneva, 1954* (Princeton: Princeton University Press, 1969), pp. 65, 97.

[d] Since some men appear more than once, and since their views at different times are probably not related randomly, a null hypothesis imaginary base rate of random distribution (50/50) is probably slightly too liberal, although by an unknown amount.

numbers of other people (as was true of President Lyndon Johnson) or did
he prefer relative isolation (Secretary Dulles, for example, would go with his
wife to an isolated island away from telephones and other people)? A very
extraverted man was one who was "emotionally outgoing, loves crowds.
Enjoys contacts with many kinds of people. Leisure time spent with
people." A very introverted subject was one described as "cold, icy, or
aloof or acutely shy. Few close friends. Leisure time spent away from
people."

An ideal personality assessment would be made by trained observers
using explicit criteria, working independently of one another, and without
prior knowledge of policy attitudes. This ideal was met only partially in the
available source material—in particular, most writers had a prior knowledge
of policy decisions; there was a tendency toward rating interdependence,
with later scholars partially relying on the work of earlier writers; and
there was a tendency toward impressionism, a lack of rigorous detailing of
specific instances which led to a generalization. Finally, the high degree of
consensus in this study might have resulted from bias in my own excerpt-
ing. For all of these reasons it is important to have an independent check.

Fortunately, a partial check is possible. Donley and Winter scored inaugural addresses (which occurred, of course, prior to later policy decisions) of 11 presidents for achievement and power motivation.[7] On this
subsample correlations with the present dominance ratings were .54
($p < .05$) for power motivation and .77 ($p < .01$) for achievement motivations. Such significant correlations are evidence that the present ratings are
reasonably valid. The high degree of consensus among coders and across related methods occurs, I think, because these were all public men much
talked about and observed (hence a consensus about them in the present
ratings) and because differences among them were quite marked.

I do not want to leave the impression, however, that the rating task was
entirely straightforward. While generally successful, the effort to disguise
identities was not wholly effective since both raters were political scientists (although not specialists in diplomatic history) and had some knowledge of the men in question: Franklin Roosevelt and Theodore Roosevelt
were each recognized by one rater.[8] In addition, there was considerable
difficulty in rating Harry Truman since he was generally egalitarian but

Table 6.3

An Inventory of Policy Disagreements: Inclusionary Policies Toward the Soviet
Union and the Soviet Bloc (Hypothesis 2)

Subjects	Description
1 Harding vs. Hughes, Hoover	Hughes and Hoover opposed Harding's desire to recognize and increase trade with the Soviet Union.
2 Eisenhower vs. Dulles	Dulles was cool toward Eisenhower's Open Skies inspection plan.
3 Eisenhower vs. Dulles	Dulles was reluctant about Eisenhower's Atoms for Peace initiative.
4 Eisenhower vs. Dulles	Eisenhower was more drawn toward summit conference with Soviet leaders than was Dulles.
5 Dulles vs. Stevenson	Stevenson was consistently more willing than Dulles to negotiate differences with the Soviet Union.
6 Eisenhower vs. Herter	Herter had grave doubts about Eisenhower's desire for a September 1959 summit meeting with Khrushchev.[a]
7 Kennedy, Acheson vs. Stevenson	Stevenson favored early negotiating rather than confrontation in the 1961 Berlin crisis.
8 Kennedy, Acheson vs. Stevenson	Stevenson favored early negotiations rather than confrontation during the Cuban missile crisis.
9 Johnson, Kennedy vs. Rusk	LBJ and JFK were more inclined toward building bridges with Eastern Europe and negotiating with the Soviet Union (e.g., test ban, disarmament initiation); Rusk was more cautious and dubious.

[a] Later in his study Noble comments that Herter "approved" of a Khrushchev visit.
(p. 291).
[b] For mean extraversion scores see notes to table 6.2.
[c] See note d to table 6.2.
[d] Dropping men not holding formal offices eliminates 3 comparisons (1 each in cases
5, 7, and 8) leaving 8 supportive and 2 opposing cases or 80% agreement ($p \approx .05$)

References	Number Consistent with Hypothesis[b]	Number Not Consistent with Hypothesis[b]
Robert K. Murray, *The Harding Era* (Minneapolis: University of Minnesota Press, 1969), pp. 348–354.	2	0
Sherman Adams, *First-Hand Report* (New York: Harper, 1961), p. 87.	1	0
Ibid., p. 112.	1	0
Ibid., p. 88; E.J. Hughes, *The Ordeal of Power* (New York: Atheneum, 1963), p. 207.	1	0
H. Muller, *Adlai Stevenson: A Study of Values* (New York: Harper and Row, 1967), pp. 154–155.	1	0
G. Bernard Noble, *Christian Herter* (New York: Cooper Square, 1970), p. 78; S. F. Bemis (ed.), *The American Secretaries of State and Their Diplomacy,* vol. 18.	1	0
See references for entries 23 and 24, table 6.2.	1	1
See references for entries 25 and 26, table 6.2.	1	1
Arthur M. Schlesinger, Jr., *A Thousand Days* (Boston: Houghton Mifflin, 1965), p. 285; P. Geyelin, *Lyndon B. Johnson and the World* (New York: Praeger, 1966), p. 83.	2	0
Totals	11	2
Percentages[c]	84.6%	15.4%
Probability[d]	$p < .002$	

fired General Douglas MacArthur for asserting too much independence. My own feeling was that this reflected a habitual low dominance on Truman's part, a tendency which produced such later problems that he was forced to act. The judges seemed to feel the same way, although with some misgivings—and it is appropriate to note that Donley and Winter do give Truman a high relative score for power motivation. Another complex case was Eisenhower, who asserted himself strongly in establishing procedures under which his key subordinates made major decisions. He is scored low here because the rating scales assessed assertion over policy *content,* although clearly there is another, *procedural,* sense in which Eisenhower was very much in charge. Herbert Hoover also was complex: he tended to be very dominant over policy initiatives intellectually, although he was a tolerant and egalitarian man who kept in office a secretary of state (Stimson) with whom he often disagreed fundamentally and strongly. Hoover is scored moderately high on dominance here, although it should be noted that a single rating scale collapses this distinction between intellectual and interpersonal dominance.

There is a final and important methodological point. When I began this study I was not totally ignorant of American foreign policy, and I knew a substantial amount about personalities and policies since World War II. It was this knowledge which helped convince me that interpersonal generalization theory was a good candidate for testing, and I used this knowledge, as well as previous studies, to specify the hypotheses and devise the rating criteria to capture what I thought would be the operative personality traits. I did not know in detail what all the evidence would show (especially that for the period prior to World War II) but I have accordingly been cautious to avoid counting too many recent cases on related issues (e.g., of Dulles-Kennan or Dulles-Stevenson disagreements) I knew in advance would support the hypotheses. The very knowledge that led me to spend time on the study and which helped me to design it also tends to undermine the characterization of the study as a completely scientific test. This problem, of course, is not unique to this study but pervades all studies of well-known events. Any retrospective study of events of which the researcher has prior knowledge is tainted; indeed the more he is an expert in his field the less scientifically definitive any explanatory study he conducts will be, and the more any ultimate theoretical verification must depend upon parallel investigations (e.g., the State Department study) using a different sample. The present study is no exception to this caveat.

Actual personality ratings employed 10-point scales, and hypotheses were tested using numerical scores. These are reported in the notes to table 6.2. However, for ease of visual presentation the 36 subjects are placed in one of 16 cells in table 6.1.

Two hypotheses were derived from interpersonal generalization theory to test for a systematic link between personality differences and policy differences. The first hypothesis was readily suggested by previous research in the Christiansen tradition; the second was my own related guess of a possible linkage.

Hypothesis

1. In cases of disagreement on the following aspects of the advocacy of force those scoring *higher* on dominance will be *advocating* the threat or use of military force, military intervention, ultimata, and the military occupation of other countries and *opposing* moves toward disarmament and arbitration agreements when compared with those scoring lower on dominance.

Hypothesis

2. In cases involving disagreement about policy toward the Soviet Union or the Soviet Bloc, those scored as *more extraverted* will advocate cooperative, inclusive policies—recognition, more trade, summit conferences, negotiations to resolve differences—when compared with those scored as more introverted.

Case Selection and the Logic of Inference

Policy disagreements were scored by myself from the same sources consulted to obtain material for personality ratings. To eliminate some alternative explanations, intra-elite personality disagreements were usually scored only when the individuals involved actually held office in the administration in power. However, to give additional coverage, a small number of individuals were also included if they were not in office at the time but appeared to differ sincerely rather than as a tactic to gain advantage in domestic political contests. The main consequence of this extended coding was to lengthen the coverage for President Theodore Roosevelt, secretaries Root and Acheson, and advisers Kennan and Stevenson. Such additional cases did not bias the results of the tests (see notes to tables 6.2 and 6.3).

An additional restriction in coding was to limit cases to those where it seemed clear that the individual involved had access to the relevant information. The chief exclusion was the comparison between Franklin Roosevelt and Secretary Hull (whom FDR had appointed for domestic political reasons and did not usually keep fully informed).

I chose to be conservative, as I noted earlier, in coding a series of disagreements on related issues rather than risk reporting a test more heavily weighted by a few individuals of whom I had detailed prior knowledge. In all of these series of cases (with the possible exception of Secretary Stimson's disagreements with the slightly more dominant and pacific President Hoover), this coding decision worked to lower the number of cases consistent with hypothesis 1.

The recorded disagreements are presented in tables 6.2 and 6.3. In all, there were 49 disagreements scored on issues related to force, 13 disagreements scored on issues involving initiatives to "build bridges" with the Soviet Union.

Of course, methodological questions may be raised against this particular list of cases. Is this a comprehensive listing of all disagreements among these participants between 1898 and 1968? If not, is the given list biased, especially considering my prior knowledge of the two hypotheses under investigation?

It cannot be maintained that this is a comprehensive list. It is doubtful that all disagreements were recorded by participants or that they all found their way from private papers to published accounts. Also, the historical literature is somewhat uneven and one has the suspicion that some administrations are more exhaustively reported upon than others. Nevertheless, intra-administration disagreement has been a prominent topic in the literature, and I would be surprised if marked disagreements on the use of force have gone unrecorded.

Granted that the list might be incomplete, could it be *biased* uncon-

sciously in favor of the hypotheses? Yes, it could. I sought to deal with this
possibility in two ways: first, by circulating an early version of my manuscript to six political scientists and diplomatic historians; and second, by
using an independent coder ignorant of the hypotheses to recode the single
most comprehensive source of personal views, Graebner's collection, *An
Uncertain Tradition: American Secretaries of State in the Twentieth Century.*[9]

None of the professionals felt able to certify the comprehensiveness of
the listing. But their comments, along with the independent coding of the
Graebner volume, were useful and did identify 3 cases, totalling 5 disagreements, to add to the original 44 coded for hypothesis 1.

One cannot claim that these procedures are exhaustive, but only that
they are reasonably thorough given the available resources. The ideal alternative would be to enlist a team of diplomatic historians for several years
of work in archives and private papers without telling them the hypotheses
under investigation. But given these checks to eliminate coding bias unwit-
tingly favorable to the hypotheses, and given the high percentages of cases
supporting the hypotheses, it seems unlikely that bias in favor of the
theory is undetected on such a scale as would alter the conclusions reported here, at least in the case of the large N for hypothesis 1.

However, the reviewers, especially the diplomatic historians, did raise
queries that deserve discussion. One diplomatic historian objected to the
inclusion of President McKinley's initial opposition to the Spanish-American War on the ground that McKinley eventually acceded to it. (I believe
McKinley's early opposition is a reasonable case to include—he opposed
the war and felt pressured into it.)

Pervasive and sometimes strong objections were both the direct assertion that factors other than personality differences (especially differences
in cognitive beliefs) explained the observed disagreement and the "anomaly" that high dominance men did not consistently favor force in all cases
and that low dominance men sometimes joined high dominance men in
advocating force in some cases. These objections clarify what is being
tested here. First, there is no claim that different cognitive beliefs are uncorrelated with different policies. It is obvious from the words of the men
themselves that different choices *are* justified in a rationalist way. The
relevant question investigated in this study is only whether the different

cognitive justifications that are typically engaged and reported by participants and diplomatic historians might also be considered manifestations
of deeper differences in personality.

Another way to put the question is to ask whether one needs first to
study each individual case and rule out all plausible alternative explanations before including that case and concluding that a novel general theory
built on such cases is valid? I think not. Such ruling out of alternative explanations in the specific case is probably impossible since, as the existent
historiography demonstrates, plausible rationalist alternatives (for example)
are already possible. What the large-*N* study (49 cases for hypothesis 1)
does is increase the confidence with which one can go back to these individual historical cases and make the interpretation of such cases less ambiguous by suggesting more weight be given to relevant psychodynamic considerations. But, of course, the fact that any one single case is *consistent*
with the present theory does not *prove* that the case is explained by the
theory; it only creates a presumption in favor of including an explanation
at the personal psychodynamic level of analysis.

My own working image of policy decisions is that behavior is multiply
determined, and a variety of forces and considerations, both arising from
the individual and from the specific situation, interact (reinforcing, mod-
ifying, or opposing each other) to produce a decision. It is not a theoretical contradiction that, in response to one situation, a high dominance man
would, *on balance,* decide *against* force while a different situation would
give more obvious and freer expression to one of his many personal motivations. I am seeking to explain a direction in interpersonal variation *about
a mean* in problematic situations (problematic by definition—i.e., those
producing intra-elite disagreement), when this range of variation already
encompasses observed advocacy and opposition to a specific policy; what
is being tested is *not* a theory which accounts for the mean, for all the
other factors (situational and otherwise) which produce a foreign policy.
(And I am *not* advancing here a theory of which foreign policy situations
are sufficiently ambiguous to yield a crucial role for personality in the
policy response.)

Another important alternative explanation is that dominance ratings merely reflect role-appropriate behavior, rather than personality traits. There is a possibility that presidents are scored as more dominant or extraverted than secretaries, or that high dominance is an artifact of growing administrative responsibility as this has increased since the turn of the century. If so, then the personality measures may not truly assess individual motives.

A test of these objections is possible. If we exclude advisers House, Hopkins, Kennan, and Stevenson we have an N of 32. Of the most dominant 16, six are presidents (Johnson, FDR, Wilson, TR, Hoover, Kennedy) and 10 are secretaries. Of the remaining 16, the same number (six) are presidents (Truman, Taft, McKinley, Eisenhower, Harding, Coolidge) and 10 are secretaries. There is no general tendency for presidents to be more dominant over subordinates than secretaries. But it is true that the top six include five presidents (Johnson, FDR, Wilson, TR, Hoover) and only one secretary (Dulles), an unlikely occurrence by chance. Thus it is true that extremely dominant men tend to become presidents rather than secretaries, but there is no general confounding of presidential role with dominance rating, and the hypothesis that these ratings are merely a function of role can be ruled out.

Of the 12 presidents, are the more recent more likely to be scored as highly dominant? Of the four presidents included since World War II, two are in the more dominant half (Johnson and Kennedy), two are in the less dominant half (Truman and Eisenhower). Of the eight presidents included prior to World War II, four are in the more dominant half (TR, Wilson, Hoover, FDR), four are in the less dominant half (McKinley, Coolidge, Harding, Taft). There is no tendency for post–World War II presidents to be more dominant over subordinates.

Of the twenty secretaries, are the more recent scored as more dominant? Of the seven recent secretaries, four are in the top 10 on dominance (Dulles, Byrnes, Acheson, Stettinius). Of the 13 prior to or during World War II, six (Hughes, Stimson, Hall, Root, Lansing, Bryan) are in the top 10 on dominance. The comparison of 4/7 with 6/13 shows only a slight (and not statistically significant) tendency for higher dominance men to be secretaries since World War II. Thus there is no general correlation of time

period with dominance rating for the secretaries, and the hypothesis that
personality ratings are confounded by increasing role requirements for
dominance can be ruled out in this case as well.

However, there is evidence that different role requirements could affect the measure of extraversion. Of 12 presidents, nine are in the top half
of the extraversion rankings and only three are in the bottom half. Of the
20 secretaries, only seven are in the top half of the extraversion ranking
and 13 are in the bottom half. So secretaries tend to be scored as more introverted, presidents as more extraverted. The question is whether this is
because of true *personality* differences or because of *role* differences. My
own inclination, based on the fact that occupants of both the presidential
and secretarial roles have shown varying behaviors (e.g., presidents Wilson,
Coolidge, and Hoover were quite introverted) is to attribute such scores
exclusively to personality variations, especially so because the rating scale
(reproduced in the notes to table 6.2) placed weight on use of leisure time
and degree of warmth rather than on role-specific behavior like presidential campaign activities and handshaking.

Results

Results of the analysis of the data are presented in tables 6.2 and 6.3. If
one accepts the personality scoring as valid, and if one accepts the cases
presented as an unbiased listing, they show strong and statistically significant support for both hypotheses 1 and 2. In 78% of the cases involving
issues of the use of force the difference along a personality dimension—
everyday dominance of subordinates—is consistent with (and, interpersonal
generalization theory would argue, explains) the observed direction of policy disagreement. In 86.6% of the cases involving issues of inclusionary initiative toward the Soviet Union or Soviet bloc the difference along a
second personality dimension—extraversion—is consistent with (explains)
the observed direction of policy disagreement.

These percentages are unusually high for a single variable in social
science research, and it will be well to look at the cases again to see how
sensitive the analysis is to various aspects of their makeup.

The most obvious fact about the force cases is the strong support given to hypothesis 1 by cases involving Theodore Roosevelt. Out of 10 instances amounting to 15 disagreements, Roosevelt's high dominance score and policy views give support to the theory in 13. Removing Roosevelt leaves $38 - 13 = 25$ cases in support and $11 - 2 = 9$ opposed: 74% support, only a slight change.

A second and more subtle characteristic is discussed in a footnote to table 6.2. Since I assumed there were multiple intra-administration forces making for policy agreement, I believed it was plausible, when indicated by historians, to think of some men as architects and others as "going along." Hence, I scored disagreements only between an outside critic and a principal policy architect, not between a dissenter or outside critic and those members of an administration who tended usually to defer in most areas of foreign policy to a principal architect. This means, for example, (in the post–World War II period) that dissents by Kennan are scored against Acheson but not against Truman, that dissents by Kennan and Acheson are scored against Dulles rather than Eisenhower, against Johnson or Kennedy rather than Rusk. But Kennan, Acheson, and Stevenson are scored as more dominant than Eisenhower or Rusk; if the "going along" category were to be disallowed, the picture becomes less supportive of hypothesis 1: in case 1, table 6.2, a Roosevelt-Day disagreement would be confirming; but in case 7 the Root-Taft disagreement would be disconfirming; in case 17 there would be a disconfirming instance where a Rusk (Assistant Secretary of State) -Kennan disagreement is counter to the theory. In case 18 a Truman-Kennan disagreement would be confirming but a Kennan-Eisenhower disagreement would be disconfirming. In case 20 the Acheson-Eisenhower disagreement would be disconfirming, but in case 21 it would be confirming. In case 23 the Acheson-Rusk disagreement would be confirming. In case 24 the Stevenson-Rusk disagreement would be disconfirming. In case 25 the Acheson-Rusk disagreement would be confirming. In case 26 the Stevenson-Rusk disagreement would be disconfirming. In case 27, the Rusk-Kennan disagreement would be disconfirming. In case 28 the Rusk-Kennan disagreement would be disconfirming. So, disallowing the "going along" category would add 13 comparisons of which 5 would be confirming and 8 disconfirming. This would change the totals to 43 confirming cases and 19 disconfirming cases or 69% agreement—still statistically significant.

I would argue, however, that the "going along" category is realistic, and should be retained. The traditional historian's judgments that Day, Truman, Eisenhower, and Rusk often took a back seat is supported by their ratings as being of lower dominance. But it is true, in general, that "principal policy architects" tend to be high dominance men. And those who "go along" tend to be of lower dominance. So, excluding low dominance men who agree to the use of force does increase slightly the number of confirming cases.

One might wish as well to drop the confirming Robert Bacon citations in cases 4, 8, and 9 on the argument that he had to dissent because his superior Root dissented. My impression of Bacon is that he was more an independent actor than a lackey of Root. But support for the theory would not be significantly reduced by removing these cases.

From the earlier discussion there still is one important rival hypothesis, not ruled out by the research design, to be considered; namely, that secretaries of state "role specialize" in advocating nonmilitary options. If we take the 20 disagreements involving a secretary of state, this turns out not to be the case: in 10 (or 50%) the secretary did oppose the threat or use of force (numbers 2, 3, 4, 5, 6, 8, 9, 12, 21, 22) but in 10 (50%) (numbers 7, 10, 13, 14, 15, 16, 17, 18, 19, 20) he was an advocate. There is, then, no general tendency for differences in these intra-administration roles to affect the observed results. This hypothesis for explaining these findings can be excluded.

An Analysis of Discrepant Cases

There are, of course, discrepant cases. Each could be considered in the search for additional variables. But, since the major interest here is exploring the viability of an interpersonal generalization explanation, let me suggest one possible variable, marked extrapunitiveness, that retrospectively seems important in the relation between interpersonal dominance and a tendency to be inclined toward the use of force. I would nominate this variable as a candidate for consideration by future researchers working with other data bases. My reasoning is as follows: in two of the eleven discrepant cases the subjects (President Hoover and Secretary Stimson) disagreed in the opposite direction than was predicted by interpersonal generalization theory. Hoover, scored slightly more dominant than Stimson, opposed the Secretary's desire to "put teeth" into the Kellogg-Briand pact by invoking economic sanctions against Japanese aggression in Manchuria. Stimson also opposed disarmament proposals which Hoover advocated. In a third case, former Secretary Elihu Root disagreed with an ultimatum issued to Chile by Secretary Knox. In other cases, former President Theodore Roosevelt, scored exactly as dominant as President Wilson, was critical of Wilson's "feeble" Mexican policies and Wilson's reluctance to enter World War I at an earlier date. Two additional cases found the slightly less dominant former Secretary of State Dean Acheson urging a harder line in the 1961 Berlin crisis and disagreeing with President Kennedy's decision to use a quarantine rather than an air strike during the Cuban missile crisis.

In each of these seven cases the men involved are close to each other on the rating scales. A more complete conceptualization of interpersonal dominance would probably yield a reversal of the relative positions here, so that these cases would, as well, support interpersonal generalization theory. In particular, special weight to tendencies to be extrapunitive or to "enjoy a good fight" would increase the dominance ratings of Theodore Roosevelt, Philander Knox, Henry Stimson, and Dean Acheson. All of these men were somewhat more noted for these characteristics than were Elihu Root, Woodrow Wilson, Herbert Hoover, and John Kennedy. For example, Theodore Roosevelt was always sounding off against someone or something. Elihu Root thought Knox's temper was decisive in the Chilean case:

Knox was a peppery sort of fellow. He got mad very easily. He did mix into things too much. He got mad at that old pelter of a case (the Alsop claim against Chile); that made no end of trouble. . . . The arbitration practically decided in favor of Chile in an amount she was ready to pay. Without saying a word to anybody, Knox took it up and gave them an ultimatum—ten days.[10]

Secretary Stimson was noted for his outbursts of temper: he would oc-

casionally have fits of anger in which he threw books and papers at his
secretary. Acheson was noted for his studied arrogance, his rapier wit,
his aversion to "suffering fools gladly," his liking for a good fight. By
contrast Elihu Root and Herbert Hoover were highly self-controlled, generally even-tempered, and disinclined to devastate an opponent. Wilson
was a fighter—but less drawn to it as a pastime than the Rough Rider. Kennedy, I think, was less inclined than Acheson to enjoy a good scrap, more
interested simply in winning.

Still, even if these modifications were made, interpersonal generalization theory as formulated here would not explain all of the disagreements.
There would be four cases (two involving Lansing and World War I, an
Acheson-Dulles disagreement where Acheson wanted a harder line in Berlin in 1958, and George Kennan's advocacy of American troop movements
to Europe at the time of the Soviet invasion of Czechoslovakia) which
would still not be explained by this single variable.

Extensions

Until this point, to rule out alternative hypotheses, comparisons among
men have been restricted to assessing the direction of their differences at
the same point in time. But the two policy tendencies studied may interact in specific situations, and collapsing the earlier 16-cell array of subjects
into a four-fold table (table 6.4) gives a basis for speculating about a more
general psychological typology of orientations toward America's role in
the international political system. Since my view of policy making is that
multiple personality and situational factors interact, I suspect that such a
typology may ultimately be more informative than single bivariate hypotheses in the broader task of giving an empathetic account of the personal coherence which may underlie a man's policies. It is obvious, for
example, that men with different personality traits could favor similar
policies—if so, however, their rationales may still differ; and one point of
the exercise is to provide some general impression of what these differences may be. In each of the four cells (which I have labeled with a summary word or phrase) there may be one or two men who do not fit the
generalizations offered here—I was guided primarily by the men in the ex-

Table 6.4

A Typology of Orientations to the International Political System

	Introvert	Extravert
	Bloc (Excluding) Leaders	**World (Integrating) Leaders**
High Dominance (Reshape)	Dulles, Wilson, Hoover, Hughes, Stimson, Acheson, House, Hull, Root.	Johnson, TR, FDR, Byrnes, Hopkins, Kennedy
	Maintainers	**Conciliators**
Low Dominance (Persevere)	Herter, Kennan, Marshall, Colby, Knox, Lansing, Coolidge, Day, Sherman, Kellogg, Rusk	Bacon, McKinley, Stettinius, Stevenson, Truman, Bryan, Taft, Eisenhower, Hay, Harding

This typology is derived by collapsing the categories of table 6.1. Characterizations are better thought of as continua than dichotomies. Dulles and Wilson, for example, are more the "ideal type" Bloc Leaders, as are the men from the other corners of the original 16-cell array.

treme (original corner) cells. And there is obviously too small an *N* in each cell for any systematic test or study to be conducted conclusively. It will probably be another century or more before there are a sufficient number of subjects to make generalizations or tests with statistical rigor. But for the reader who is not averse to impressions, let me propose the following ideas.

The *Bloc Leaders* and the *World Leaders* are men who are rated high in their tendencies to dominate their subordinates in their everyday lives. They differ from one another in their degree of introversion or extraversion. An example of a Bloc Leader (high dominance introvert) would be Secretary of State John Foster Dulles; an example of a World Leader (high dominance extravert) would be President Theodore Roosevelt.

The Bloc Leaders tend to divide the world, in their thought, between the moral values they think it ought to exhibit and the forces opposed to this vision. They tend to have a strongly moralistic, almost Manichean, view of this dichotomy. They may be described as stubborn and tenacious. They seek to reshape the world in accordance with their personal vision, and their foreign policies are often characterized by the tenaciousness with which they advance one central idea. Examples would be Woodrow Wilson's "puritanical" Mexican policies and his advocacy of a League of Nations, Elihu Root's dogged efforts to negotiate arbitration treaties and strengthen the rule of international law, Charles Evans Hughes' advocacy of the World Court, Herbert Hoover's pursuit of disarmament, Secretary Hull's determined efforts for reciprocal free trade, and Acheson's and Dulles' dominant concern with containing what they perceived as the Communist menace.

The World Leaders seem to want to be leaders of the entire world rather than just the bloc of the ideologically acceptable. They too have a tendency to use military force. In general they are more flexible and pragmatic, more varied in the range of foreign policy initiatives. They want to lead rather than contain. They advocate change, seek to stir up things globally—whether Theodore Roosevelt getting his hand into arbitrations to end the Russo-Japanese War, the Algeciras Conference, and so forth; Franklin Roosevelt planning for the Four Policemen in the post–World War II period; President Kennedy's Alliance for Progress, Peace Corps,

Congo operation, dispatch of advisers to South Vietnam, and initiation of efforts toward rapprochement with the Soviet Union; Lyndon Johnson's efforts in building bridges with Eastern Europe, the Glassboro summit, the SALT talk initiatives. The Bloc Leaders seem relatively preoccupied with themes of *exclusion,* the establishment of institutions or principles to keep potentially disruptive forces in check. The World Leaders, while they share some of the same concerns, are relatively more interested in *inclusion,* initiating programs and institutions for worldwide leadership and cooperative advance on a wide range of issues.

The men of low interpersonal dominance, the *Maintainers* and the *Conciliators,* are less inclined toward willful and major projects for reshaping the world political system. One element of this (which has already been documented) is their lower inclination to advocate the use of military force. Yet these latter groups also differ significantly from one another.

The men of low interpersonal dominance who are introverted, the Maintainers, evidence a common theme in their foreign policy orientations: a holding action for the status quo.[11] An extreme case is Calvin Coolidge, who mentions not one word about foreign policy in his autobiography—he was content to leave it in the custody of his secretary of state. Somewhat more representative of this group of men is Dean Rusk, of whom Arthur Schlesinger comments:

If the problem were an old one, he was generally in favor of continuing what Herter or Dulles or Acheson had done before him. If the problem were new, it was generally impossible to know what he thought.[12]

Another example would be Secretary Kellogg, who, as one scholar notes, "kept the shop running, but few new goods were put on the shelves." I think George Kennan is exemplary of this group as well—his emphasis, for the past 30 years, has centered on maintaining those four out of five key industrial areas of the world now in friendly hands in those hands.

In the final category are the Conciliators, the extraverted men who seek relatively egalitarian relations with their nominal subordinates. My impression is that they tend to respond to circumstances with the sympathetic hope that accommodations can be negotiated. They are not inclined to reshape the world in accordance with a grand vision. But they do seem less comfortable with only the status quo than are the Maintainers. They seem more flexible, more hopeful, more open to change. They also seem—in historical perspective—to lack consistent and strong willpower, to be humane but peripheral footnotes. They are the Adlai Stevensons of history. They are backed into a Spanish American War (McKinley); major policy carries the imprint of a Hughes, Acheson, or Dulles (rather than of a Harding, Truman, or Eisenhower); they languish unhappily at the United Nations during the Vietnam War (Stevenson). Many of their own policy initiatives seem quickly lost: Hay's paper Open Door policy in China, Eisenhower's Open Skies and Atoms for Peace plans.

To my mind, a striking cleavage among all of these men occurs between the introverts and the extraverts. The introverts seem to be drawn to the ideal of a world system operating by *impersonal mechanisms*. During the interwar (post–World War I) swing of the international political system into legalism, men of this persuasion inclined to a superstructure of international law. At other times a balance of power has been their normative model. But, whether the vision has been alliance of the righteous or separate geographical spheres of influence, the underlying theme has been an ideal of boundaries and impersonal mechanisms for maintaining those boundaries. It is as though these men sought a world order that was less personally engaging, more impersonally and automatically controlled. By contrast, the extraverts seem to transcend (if that is the correct word) the view of a world order dependent only upon a balance of power. They are more interested in involvement and collaboration. A paradigmatic case of similar policies favored for these different reasons would be the differing emphases of President Wilson and Secretary Stettinius. Wilson saw the League of Nations as dealing with international aggression by invoking moral rules and sanctions against the transgressor. Secretary Stettinius saw the United Nations operating more as a forum for discussion and negotiation. In the first case a cold, aloof, introverted man sought a mechanism to impose a solution by imposing a principle. In the second case a warm, egalitarian, extraverted man sought an institution for mutual give-and-take.

Conclusions, and a Proposed Test

Psychohistorical studies have their share of methodological problems. But by existing standards the present study, I would submit, holds its own, and the risk of error in accepting its main conclusions is small. The personality ratings are based on explicit criteria, they converge with available indepen- dent measures of similar traits, and their variation is not a product of the subject's role. The listing of cases, while extensive, may not be exhaustive; but it did pass several independent checks for bias. The design, by making comparisons at the same point in time, ruled out major alternative explan- ations, and the data ruled out the remaining rival hypothesis of policy view as a function of intra-administration role. The data are strongly supportive of both hypotheses (especially of hypothesis 1), and their statistical signi- ficance is markedly insensitive to various objections. And the theory is consistent with other findings using other subjects—in particular, with the State Department study, which documented interpersonal generalization processes among a random sample of American diplomats.

Most readers cannot, of course, verify for themselves the accuracy of all the historical details in this study. But the reader can observe to see whether the theories themselves are accurate predictors. Let me offer a test: the major memoirs of the Nixon administration (Nixon, Haldeman, Kissinger, Ehrlichman, Rogers) have not yet appeared as this book goes to press, and the reader can use them to see whether they verify the theories. While many of the foreign policies of the Nixon administration continued previous policies or were conditioned by international situations, this book predicts what these memoirs will document about interpersonal differences: *if* there was marked disagreement on the use of force, then Secretary of State Rogers, a low dominance man, will have dissented from the militar- istic policies (e.g., the Cambodian invasion, the Christmas bombing of Hanoi) toward which the two high dominance men (Nixon and Kissinger) were more favorable. And *if* there was marked disagreement over the open- ing to China and détente, a more extraverted man like Rogers will have been favorable earlier than the moderate extravert (Kissinger) or the intro- vert (Nixon)—and Kissinger will have persuaded Nixon rather than the re- verse. Moreover, agreement on the China or détente initiatives would, if it occurred, have been supported from different rationales: by Kissinger and Nixon more out of balance of power rationales, by Rogers more from a hopeful desire to have friendly relations.

One might be reassured if rational choice prevailed in American foreign policy decision making, but that view now appears, in major ways, to be it-self a fantasy. The good reasons which are sold to the public—and which have been bought by some diplomatic historians and political scientists—do not exhaust the repertoire of reasons behind, and in some cases may not be the most important reasons behind, policy decisions. Lasswell's pioneer-ing formulation is at least partially correct: personal motives (e.g., to dom-inate) are systematically displaced onto policy issues with the results (e.g., American war against a small country) rationalized as being in the nation's interest.[13] And we may also conclude that the American political system does have a tendency to elevate to high office men who are prone to use military force.

The State Department and Historical Studies in Perspective

Research usually places a social scientist in two conflicting roles; while act-ing as a critic of his own and previous researchers' attempts to discern truth amidst the complexity of life, he is also trying to make a strong case that, after all, *he* at least has arrived in *his* research at some unassailable conclu-sion. The perfect study—one conducted over several decades and based on enormous quantities of personal data (including depth interviews) from politicians, top level political appointees, and career ambassadors, the use of multiple methods to assess individuals—will have to await the interest and cooperation of top political elites, a willingness to be skeptical of the rationality they mistakenly attribute to their own judgment.[14] Neverthe-less, the State Department and historical studies, each falling short of this ideal, converge strongly, with different methods and subjects, on a con-sistent picture that personality predispositions do shape individual elite policy preferences and can decisively shape America's major foreign poli-cies. And I would claim the hard evidence for this proposition is now far better than for the skeptical hypothesis that such effects are inconsequen-tial or nonexistent. On the basis of the evidence assembled and analyzed here, I think the burden of proof shifts and that foreign policy makers in America and elsewhere face the issue of establishing that their future de-cisions for war or peace are fully based only on truly national and objec-tive considerations, rather than expressing mere rationalizations of private emotional predispositions.

7 Summary: Sources of Error and War

A world of science and great machines is still a world of men.

David Lilienthal

In this concluding chapter I will undertake four tasks. First, I will draw together the findings from previous chapters and show their convergence with the evidence from projective tests detailing how emotional processes affect the imaginative experiments decision makers use to conceive the world and select satisfactory policy. Second, I will offer a brief summary of the main points of the "leader's personality" theory of decision making suggested by the evidence. Third, I will consider whether the psychological insights from this research offer any guidance to people who wish to reduce foreign policy errors or the incidence of war. Finally, I will offer concluding remarks about the seriousness of the problem addressed in this book, namely the unnecessary and avoidable deaths of the victims of the commonplace features of political psychology I have studied.

International Politics as a Projective Test

As we have seen, American foreign policy is not grounded exclusively in objective reality. Instead, the shapers of that policy, like all men, react partly intuitively to the world; and they adopt the most subjectively plausible self-expressive responses to the situations in which they find themselves. Self-expression and projective intuition converge to form a self-deceptive pseudorationality. While there is always the possibility of fortuitous agreement between predispositions and the true structure of international politics, such a decision-making process will often not be reliable.

This is, of course, not a complete characterization of the thought processes brought to bear on foreign policy questions. But, as we have seen, self-expression and projective intuition can decisively tip the balance of major decisions.

These findings accord with much additional evidence developed by social scientists about the functioning of the mind when it is presented with inadequate objective data.[1] If you show a man a picture of other people and ask him to tell you a story he will, without much difficulty, tell you a great deal which extends beyond the surface facts of the picture itself. He will readily imagine and tell you about the motives and feelings of different characters, perhaps tell you whether they are restless or content, trustworthy or treacherous, what they strive for or fear, whether he likes or dislikes them. Possibly he will tell you about the future that will unfold for the characters in the picture, what opposition or support they can expect, what the consequences of different actions by different characters might be.

If you provide a man with many different pictures, the themes he imagines will vary greatly (assuming that he is mentally healthy) depending on cues from the picture itself. A mother holding a peaceful baby and smiling tenderly will cue certain feelings and themes in his mind; an older and angry man behind a desk shaking his finger at a younger man will arouse other responses and suggest different themes to the storyteller.

And yet, if you consider the themes which any one man tends to supply across different pictures, you will find that his themes differ from those supplied by another storyteller and, moreover, that the themes of these different men will vary in ways that are straightforward and characteristic representations of the personality differences among them. For example, men who tend to see people as being highly concerned with power typically are men who in their own lives have high power motivation, who seek power, and who fear the use of power against them by others. Storytellers who enunciate fewer power themes turn out to have lower motivation to acquire power and less fear of the power of others in their own lives.[2] In retrospect, and viewed in context, each man's stories can be seen to reflect the confluence, in different proportions, of different aspects of his personality that are triggered by the bare and ambiguous cues presented to his objective scrutiny.

The philosopher John Dewey has provided a classic description of deliberation and decision making as an imaginative process. Deliberation, Dewey wrote, is a

Dramatic rehearsal in imagination of various competing lines of action. . . . It is an experiment in making various combinations of habits and impulses to see what the resultant action would be like if it were entered upon.[3]

What can now be added to Dewey's account is specific evidence and detail of systematic personality-based shaping of those "habits and impulses" which different men find most accessible within themselves to draw upon and use when they make decisions. Such a process appears rational on the surface, but the deep, largely unconscious sources of imaginative processes introduce an implicit, unrecognized, subjective shaping of perception and outcome.

The data from past chapters fit this theory of a convergence of self-expression and projective intuition in the imaginative processes of policy deliberation. The evidence from chapter 3 is that differences in external situations (stimuli) are a major determinant of whether the predisposition to use force is aroused, and the data in chapters 4 and 6 indicate that the tendency to employ or oppose force within each situation reflects more general personality-based differences between individuals.

That different issues or situations selectively engage different aspects of personality was found in chapter 4, and again in chapter 5.[4] For example, in chapter 4 we saw competitiveness engaged by challenges in underdeveloped countries but suppressed when the subjects faced a direct confrontation with the Soviet Union. Furthermore, the ambition to feel active and powerful increased the tendency to *use* military force but did not affect the level of war capabilities desired. And the evidence has been summarized, in chapter 5, for different patterns of personality engagement in perception: the data showed certain aspects of personality systematically engaged to create the image of the Soviet Union while the same aspects of personality were not engaged to create the different image of British foreign policy. Finally, the evidence from both chapters 4 and 5 showed that policy views and perceptions are multiply affected (sometimes in conflicting directions) by the confluence of different personality-based determinants. Thus these findings merge with the well-established literature in psychology that deals with imaginative processes. International politics is crucially a projective test.[5]

By stressing that men probably use self-expression and projective intuition in the responsible effort to make effective policy and in the service of understanding the world, I do not want to rule out the possibility that such personal involvement might be supported by other motives and considerations. Self-expression and projective intuition can create a comfortable sense of confidence (even overconfidence and a pose of arrogant omniscience), a justification for dismissing critics. There could well be important ego gratifications from the power to shape world events as an expression of oneself.[6]

Sources of Error and War

I think the evidence from the State Department and historical studies (and the ancillary evidence from studies of the general public, from cross-cultural anthropology, from Donley and Winter, and from the study of projective test behavior) clarifies five of the basic sources of error and war:
Within the decision maker are three sources:

1. The tendency to express personal motives, behavorial patterns, and fears in decisions, and especially doing so without flexibly assessing the value of this self-expression.

2. The tendency to introduce these same a priori internal structures and forces into intuitive processes to shape beliefs about external reality, again without flexibly assessing the appropriateness of these images.

3. The mind's tendency to deceive itself by using the confidence and consistency generated by these first two subjective processes as an erroneous criterion for believing its decisions are right and rational.

Beyond these three sources of error in the typical processes of a leader's mind, there is a source of error and war external to the decision maker:

4. The ambiguous, uncertain nature of international reality which makes it difficult to reliably calibrate self-expression and intuition and converts what might be a straightforward technical problem into a projective test.

Finally:

5. The fact that American elite composition—and especially presidential personalities—are generated by domestic political structures and processes which:
a. Offer no guarantee (except by fortuitous circumstance) that the personal predispositions of the most influential people will be appropriately aligned with requirements for success and realism in every situation; and

b. In the American case introduce significant ingredients (i.e., competition, ambition, dominance) which, in conjunction with the four features listed above, make fear and war more likely.

I should add that, while the mechanisms in this list increase directly the likelihood of the use of American force, their effects in other nations can also be consequential. That is, if these same mechanisms are true of the most influential leaders in a foreign country, those leaders may thereby produce situations which serve to arouse fears and military tendencies in American decision makers. For example, the ambitions of Hitler and Japanese leaders in World War II, Stalin's approval of North Korea's invasion of South Korea, Soviet Premier Khrushchev's forays in various crises, and many other cases of confrontation with America might well be instances in which the personal psychology of top foreign decision makers played a crucial role.

This complex web of self-expression and intuition would of course not be necessary if international politics could be a science instead of an art. But unfortunately it will probably remain an art: presidents will decide emotionally arousing issues in the face of ambiguous and inadequate data and with theories that can be only partially validated. And the sober, unpleasant lesson is that such conditions increase the likelihood of major error and war in the future.

I think there is another potential conclusion in these data—that there is a darker side to heroic ambition. This deserves comment because of the hope of many people for forceful leaders to bring domestic progress. While not a logical necessity, it appears from the evidence that popular leaders with heroic vision and determination may often be predisposed to extend their crusades for a better world into foreign military battle. Americans drawn to Teddy Roosevelt's trust-busting also made possible Big Stick foreign policy. People were drawn to Woodrow Wilson's heroic idealism and Mexico was invaded. They voted for the New Frontier and got the Bay of Pigs and assassination plots. They voted for the Great Society and got an escalation of the Vietnam War. And the pattern exists more dramatically for other nations: Hitler promised his people a thousand-year Reich, Napolean promised his an empire. Both failed and also left millions dead.[7]

Alternatives

Given the personalization of foreign policy at the higher levels, the question arises whether there are ways of selecting leaders who will be predisposed to act in ways that bring peace. For any one nation such a foolproof selection cannot be made without a prior agreement on the nature of international reality: if the leaders of the Soviet Union are primarily hard-line and expansionist, then selecting American leaders strongly disposed to trust and cooperation could be erroneous. In the same way the Soviet Union would be ill-advised, from the viewpoint of its national security, to select trusting and cooperative leaders if American political leaders are primarily hard-line and expansionist.

But the implications are clear for all nations taken together. A collective shift toward leaders of less personal ambition and less dominance, less competitiveness, more inclined toward trust—men gentle, kind, and modest—would increase the likelihood our world could live at peace. Yet such a shift may not be possible, since the peoples of the world cannot act in concert.

Despite the implausibility of any direct political application of these results, greater psychological understanding of themselves by elites might be salutary. By creating for decision makers an explicit metaperspective on their inherent mental processes and biased, overconfident functioning, such increased self-awareness might enlarge their capacity to use their personal predispositions more modestly and their intuitive resources more flexibly in the service of accurate empathy and successful policy.

This study, of course, is only a first step toward such sophisticated self-awareness; and it is unclear whether top political leaders would be interested in supporting more projects to increase their professional competence. Both personally and politically these might be unattractive.

There are three responses to this elite reserve. First, there is the fact of the public responsibility and trust which political leaders hold: the private selves of public leaders—their fantasies and other personality traits—manifestly affect their professional judgments, sometimes consequentially, on issues of major political importance. Hence increased self-knowledge is part of meeting standards of a responsible professionalism. It takes courage to confront this fact—but it would at least begin to approach the courage of the soldiers who leaders now ask to face death on the battlefield. I think that leaders should expect no less of themselves—and we should expect no less of them.

Second, it is not true that greater self-knowledge, as some people fear, increases neurotic soul-searching and paralyzes the capacity to act. The results of psychoanalysis and psychotherapy show rather that, if it is done well, the opposite is the case: self-awareness leads to a strengthening of the self, a deeper sense of one's values. More importantly, there is a sense of release, greater flexibility, creativity, and perspective—an inner freedom to have one's ideas challenged without feeling set upon.[8] The problem to which a research program is appropriately addressed is how to free a decision maker to bring *all* of his potential capabilities to bear on an issue, how to make empathy and intuition *flexible* rather than, as at present, locking in a man and restricting his processes of judgment and intuition. The goal is to support the creation of more fully human, sophisticated, and sensitive policy makers, not to intimidate men so they repress their feelings and function like machines.

Third, it will be necessary to create a research and educational program which is psychologically safe. It will be distressing if this book, with its public criticism, makes men reluctant to further explore their subjective processes out of fear of adverse political consequences or personal embarrassment. To succeed, a program would need to be private, conducted with a high sense of professional ethics by people of integrity. And the media would need to eschew voyeurism and the short-term sensationalism and competitive advantage to be gained from searching out and printing privileged information. But I think that arrangements could be worked out and that, moreover, an honest program in the Executive Branch would be reassuring to the American public, to foreign governments and peoples, to the Congress, useful to presidents and secretaries of state personally in meeting their responsibilities, reassuring to the news media, and reassuring, as well, to top level officials who frequently must rely on professional staffs and appointees for sound judgments and advice. And of course foreign governments could appropriately begin their own programs. Such programs would obviously have to be voluntary—both to be ethical and to meet the first requirement of a good working relationship.

I am not, of course, in a position to predict with certainty that an advanced program of research and education explicating the personal psychology of political decision making will increase the flexibility and appropriateness of self-expression and intuition. But it seems worth doing whatever can be done, and irresponsible not to address the problem directly and fully.

Concluding Remarks

This book has not been only an investigation of the resort to self-expression and intuitive processes, or only about processes of self-deception, about structural patterns of elite recruitment and their consequences, about the vicissitudes of innocence and the realistic virtues of a mature skepticism about politicians and political systems. It has been about unnecessary and avoidable death, because that is what we are talking about when we talk about decisions to use force and about erroneous judgments on issues involving force. It is a special misfortune that some of the many deaths from international violence in this century could, in principle, have been avoided; the mechanisms clarified in this book have been known to have a likely relevance to politics for at least the forty years since Harold Lasswell's pioneering investigations in his *Psychopathology and Politics* and *World Politics and Personal Insecurity*.[9,10] No one listened, at least not the people in power who could have taken to heart Lasswell's warning and clarified their own judgmental processes to avoid systematic folly. Nor am I completely confident that the world's political elites are sufficiently motivated to listen this time around. The State Department data imply that elites may have somewhat idealized images of themselves.[11] And perhaps every administration indulges itself in the vanity that it is more sophisticated than its predecessors, believing there is a bright future ahead now that they are in charge and the past is behind us.

I wish it were possible to end this book with a note of hope. But in truth I do not know whether hope is a realistic stance. Men may have the capacity to be rational, generous, and mutually cooperative, but as we face a world in which nuclear weapons and conventional armaments proliferate, it is sobering to know that the world in which they proliferate is a world of men. Human beings will decide whether or not to use them. And that necessity to trust the minds of human leaders, especially given the results of the present research, makes me uneasy.

Appendix A
Methodology of the State Department Study

Administration

Invitations to participate in the study were mailed, together with a questionnaire, to a random sample of 300 foreign service officers stationed in Washington, to the 100 military officers in the current class at the National War College (now the National Defense University), and were distributed by two contacts to 50 members of the domestic affairs section of the Office of Management and Budget.[1] Cover letters described the project in general terms and promised a report of the findings if the respondent completed and returned a separate form (this was to be returned in a separate envelope to preserve anonymity of the questionnaire itself). The State Department mailing also included a letter of introduction from David Biltchik, a foreign service officer who was head of the Face-to-Face program established by the Carnegie Endowment and the American Foreign Service Association. Follow-up letters were mailed to FSOs and military officers about a week after the first contact.[2]

The author was identified in these letters as a doctoral student associated with Yale University and holding a fellowship grant from the National Institute of Mental Health through the Yale Psychological Study of Politics program.

Sampling and Response Bias

The results of the study may be somewhat sensitive, in several respects, to details of its conduct and execution. Specifically:

1. The use of mailed questionnaires rather than personal contacts probably reduced significantly the response rate at the State Department and National War College (to 42% and 49%, respectively, compared with 74% at OMB).[3]

2. Members of the OMB staff were experiencing a temporary lull following completion of the president's budget; this and the time required to complete the lengthy questionnaire (45 minutes to an hour) probably also contributed to lower response rates at the State Department and NWC. This hypothesis was supported by the tendency of response rates to decrease (to 30%) at the higher levels (FSO-1 and FSO-2) in the State Depart-

ment. As a result, one key variable, the tendency to adopt a traditionalist view of the origins of the cold war, is probably slightly understated since this variable is associated with rank (as well as with age).

3. The questionnaire did not inquire about sensitive current issues (e.g., the SALT talks, relations with the Middle East, Vietnam, Cambodia, India, Pakistan, Chile, Taiwan, and the People's Republic of China) in favor of issues that would serve the theoretical purposes of the study for which candid responses would be more easily obtained. Nevertheless some diplomats and military officers declined to participate on the grounds it would be inappropriate for them to answer *any* questions. This attitude, which I assume may include a component of fear of the potential disapproval of one's superiors, probably means that the degree of psychological subordination to American foreign policy is understated in the results obtained. Thus the variables associated with psychological transcendence—altruism, generosity, reluctance to use force—are probably slightly less characteristic of military officers and FSOs in general than they are among those who agreed to participate.

4. It also became clear, both directly and indirectly, that some men felt deeply threatened and were, as a result, antagonistic to the study. I could not tell whether this was a result of a personal aversion to quantitative methods, to psychological probing, a mistrust of my motives, or a fear that the results—if any significant findings were obtained—might undermine the credibility of the State Department, or was a combination of these and other feelings. But a plausible guess is that those who did not respond were somewhat more mistrustful and somewhat more antagonistic than those who did participate.[4] Thus these tendencies are probably understated, and the associated tendencies to use force and to be fearful of the Soviet Union also ought to be somewhat increased if one wishes to extrapolate to all FSOs and military officers.

5. It is part of the folk wisdom of survey research (although there is little hard evidence) that individuals with low self-esteem or larger numbers of neurotic symptoms are less likely to respond voluntarily to psychological questionnaires.[5] If so, then some adjustment would also be needed in these scores and in the reported tendency to advocate the use of force.

In sum, then, those who did respond are probably not fully representative of those who did not respond. The results obtained probably overstate slightly the degree of trust, psychological transcendence, self-esteem, and mental health in these groups as a whole. And they probably understate slightly the prevalence of strong traditional views of the origins of the cold war, the fear of the Soviet Union, the tendency to use force, and overstate slightly the degree of altruism and generosity in the sample compared with those who did not respond.

History: Changes During the Course of Research

Former Ambassador John Bartlow Martin once observed that national policy can be "overtaken by events."[6] The same is true of researchers: one potential problem is that changes in the international or domestic political climate may occur while the research is in progress and diminish the comparability of results obtained at the beginning and at the end of the research period. Fortunately no such problem seemed to emerge here: the time of the study—December, 1971, to early February, 1972, was a relatively quiet period in international relations. The study commenced following the end of the latest India-Pakistan war and was concluded prior to President Nixon's previously announced trip to Peking. The only major news story was the revelation of secret transcripts by columnist Jack Anderson which showed that the administration, while officially and publicly neutral during the India-Pakistan war, was in fact ordered by President Nixon in private to "tilt toward Pakistan." However revelations of official duplicity were nothing new in Washington, and it is unlikely that such newspaper stories significantly affected the study, especially so because nothing in the study dealt with highly sensitive issues then under active discussion.[7]

Instrument-Subject Interactions: Order Effects

One problem with questionnaires is that the order of presentation of questions may introduce a halo effect that colors answers to later items; or a subject may become fatigued or otherwise affected while working his

way through the questionnaire and this may affect his answers. The trick
is to minimize the extent to which such effects generate *systematic* patterns
of response across subjects that can be mistaken for true correlations. To
deal with this problem, questionnaire items were grouped into six units on
the basis of response format, page orders within units were varied systematically, and the units were assembled in random order and then randomly
assigned to subjects. Each individual received a different order of presentation selected at random. Thus the probability was minimized that subjects
who would give a biased response to a given order would receive that order.
In addition, the order of adjective scales within the semantic differential
ratings, although constant for each object, was varied randomly across the
six objects.[8]

It is also a possibility that an individual might guess what is being investigated and alter his answer to affect what would be concluded about
him. This seems unavoidable in the case of policy questions and for several
of the perceptual scales; but for the personality scales items were inter-
mixed from other scales with identical format, or "buffer items" were included.[9]

Instrument-Subject Interactions: Clarity

An important question about the validity of the policy attitude measures
is whether the questions posed and the options provided were clear and
meshed with the naturally occurring categories of the respondents. Two
procedures were used to deal with this issue: first, an initial draft of the
questionnaire was used in a pilot study with a small group of foreign policy specialists and graduate students in international relations, and the
questionnaire was revised to eliminate any ambiguities that emerged.
Second, a tally was kept for all questionnaires to indicate those questions
which produced additional comments or qualifications by respondents.
This tally showed that only two questions prompted qualifications by
more than 2% of respondents. In one case the question about policies
toward nonexpansionist Communist governments in underdeveloped
countries provided two options, "oppose them" or "accept them." Five

FSOs who checked "accept them" felt it important to add the cautionary note "but do not encourage them."

The only significant validity problem occurred with attributions of Soviet intentions in the Middle East. To force respondents to divide between essentially a muddling-through incrementalist conception and a long-range expansionist conception, a middle-ground option of "muddling-through expansionism" was not included. Twenty-eight percent of diplomats wrote in this kind of additional option on their own and checked it. (Since some who may have preferred this option may not have written it in, the 28% is probably an underestimate and the other percentages probably are slightly overrepresented.) But the demonstrated willingness of respondents to alter options with which they did not feel comfortable provides evidence that other questions did align readily with their true attitudes.[10]

Scales—General Remarks

Most of the personality trait scales used were standard scales developed by previous researchers: the Leary Interpersonal Checklist measured dominance and hostility in interpersonal relations, competitiveness, and provided the adjective self-portraits in chapter 3. The Survey Research Center Trust in People scale (a modified version of the Rosenberg Misanthropy scale) assessed trust. The short form of the Maudsley (Eysenck) Personality Inventory measured neurotic symptoms and extraversion. Where reported in the literature these scales have test-retest reliabilities of about .70 and also display face validity.

The six objects assessed by the standard semantic differential technique (Myself, What I Would Like To Be, American Foreign Policy, Ideal American Foreign Policy, Soviet Foreign Policy, British Foreign Policy) were each rated on 20 adjective dimensions. A factor analysis (orthogonal rotation, varimax criterion) performed on the State Department random sample generated the factorial structure employed for all groups: the *evaluative* factor consisted of the adjective pairs good-bad, skillful-bungling, kind-cruel, honest-dishonest, friendly-menacing, and trusting-fearful (the

friendly-menacing scale for British and Soviet foreign policies were also
separated as single variables for further analysis); an *activity-power* factor
(interpreted as an ambition score when referring to the ideal self) consisted
of the adjective pairs: active-passive, fast-slow, moving-still, strong-weak,
hard-soft, tenacious-yielding, aggressive-defensive, leading-following, dominating-submitting, and resolute-irresolute: a *pragmatism* factor consisted
of the adjective pairs pragmatic-ideological and realistic-naive; and a *stability* factor consisted of the single adjective pair stable-changeable.[11]

Separate factor analyses of self objects (Myself, What I Would Like to
Be) compared with the four foreign policy objects in the FSO random
sample showed factor structures virtually identical with the combined
factor structure.[12] However, factor structures decomposed by object and
by group showed substantial variability across these 18 separate factor
structures—implying that the very general summary analysis used in the
text loses considerable information by forcing subtle and complex thought
into a Procustean bed. This suggests that significantly greater explanatory
power of theories dealing with personality effects on cognition and perception might be obtained with a larger data base and a multimethod strategy
which clarifies the reasons for these differing structures.[13]

Scales—Tendency to Advocate Force

It is important to emphasize that the five scenarios reported in chapter 4
were *not* a random sample of situations confronting policy makers. No
conclusion is warranted that anyone scoring 60% on this scale will tend to
advocate the use of force in 60% of all future foreign policy decisions.
Instead, the scenarios were based on recent American policy and were
constructed by an intuitive process to present situations in which the overt
use of American force would be considered a relevant option.

It is also important to emphasize that the scenarios were standardized,
specifically worded to stipulate certain beliefs on the part of the respondent, usually a belief that the use of force would be an effective policy
tool. This may have had the consequence of increasing slightly the number
of respondents who were favorable to force compared with their policy
views in an actual decision-making situation.

The internal structure of the scale deserves brief attention in three respects: reliability, undimensionality, and the potential confounding of direction with intensity in the analysis of such a Likert scale. The inter-item correlations of the five items were modest, averaging about .40. In other words, "tendency to use force" is not a strong trait in which the direction of a man's judgment can always be predicted across situations. Many factors enter into a final decision. The practical effect of this problem is that the moderate reliability of this scale means that the overall variance which *could* be explained even by a perfect theory is substantially reduced (see the discussion below on correction for attenuation and explanatory power), making the explanatory power of the results obtained (relative to that which might have been explained with greater prior knowledge and a more sophisticated scale) greater than the R^2 statistics which are reported.

One subtle aspect of the tendency to use force is illustrated by the finding that it is rather consistently affected by the same personality traits across all five scenarios, except that a possible confrontation with the Soviet Union is not affected by competitiveness while using troops in the four other scenarios is consistently affected by variations in this trait. (In the text this difference is attributed to the fact that the other four scenarios deal with underdeveloped countries. But, in truth, the 5-item scale used in the study is too preliminary to be certain that this was the operative difference).

A final problem is that the scenarios were presented as 7-point Likert scales (ranging from "strongly advocate" to "strongly oppose"). Allowing such a weight for intensity to enter into a study of the relation between affect and decision, a common practice, potentially confounds those personality traits that affect *intensity* of advocacy with those that affect *direction*. To avoid this confounding, the variable was scored to take into account only the *direction* of the policy decision (% of cases), not its intensity. This is the more circumscribed analysis reported in the text.[14]

A Note on Models

The regression results reported are the best-fit equations resulting from the following general model:

$Y = a_0 + b_1 X_1 + b_2 (\text{NWC shift}) + b_3 (\text{OMB shift}) + b_4 (\text{NWC shift}) X_1 + b_5$
(OMB shift) X_1.

The term a_0 is a derived constant, the intercept; b_i is the coefficient of the ith term; X_1 is the independent variable (scaled from 0 to 10 except for competitiveness, which is 0 or 1), Y is the dependent variable (scaled from 0 to 10 except for the tendency to use force which goes from 0% to 100% and the desired force level which goes from ½ to 2½.) The additional interaction terms were included to test whether the National War College and Office of Management and Budget respondents differed significantly from foreign service officers. The term a_0 is the estimated intercept term for *all* respondents: the "shift" factors (technically, "dummy variables") have the value of 1 when a respondent is a member of the comparison group associated with the dummy variable and the value of 0 otherwise. If the intercept term for National War College respondents differs significantly from a_0, for example, this will show up as a significant value $p(t)$ for b_2; if so, the overall intercept will be a_0 (for foreign service officers) and respondents from the Office of Management and Budget) and $a_0 + b_2$ for the respondents from the National War College. If b_3 is also significant, then the overall intercept (applicable now only for foreign service officers) will be a_0, the intercept term for respondents from the National War College will be $a_0 + b_2$, and the intercept term for respondents from the Office of Management and Budget will now be $a_0 + b_3$.

The general equation is read, similarly, for the slope of the independent variable: b_1 is the overall slope estimate for all respondents, b_4 is the shift in the overall slope estimate for NWC, b_5 is the shift in the overall slope for OMB (i.e., the NWC slope is $b_1 + b_4$: the OMB slope is $b_1 + b_5$).

In analyzing the data all of these terms were entered into the computer as *potential* terms in a best-fit model. Stepwise regression was employed to select from these terms those which made a significant contribution in increasing R^2.[15] In other words, complexity was introduced conservatively up to the point where there was no significant increase in the proportion of the variance explained by a more complex equation.

The model of the mind used in this study has been a simple one. I have imagined that there is one "generic" mind, with each individual's mind

being a snapshot of a possible configuration of this mind. The simple equations in chapters 4 and 5 have implicitly assumed that all of these snap-
shots can be treated as equivalent except for the two independent variables
under consideration. At the end of chapter 5 this simplifying assumption is
removed and the best-fit linear additive model using all of the relevant variables from the study is presented.

One problem for further research is how empathy and explanatory
power could be expanded by obtaining more data from more individuals. I
am deeply aware of the simplicity of generalizing about all individuals
taken together and I recognize that I have not differentiated among individuals in this study. There may be some individuals prone to use self-expression and projective intuitionism a great deal, others to use it little. It
would be especially useful to study this phenomenon and determine what
sorts of life experiences and professional training might contribute to
unusual clarity, flexibility, and objectivity in the use of the imagination.

In addition, it is quite plausible that the minds of different people function in different ways; the opportunity to develop and test more complex
models could increase explanatory power and insight. I have in mind the
male sexual and narcissistic fantasies and fears in the foreign policy thought
of ambitious men which, if my reading of the clinical literature of male
narcissistic striving is correct, could clarify further some especially aggres-
sion- and fear-prone dynamics in international politics.

Validity of Results—General Considerations

The most serious question about the State Department study is, "Did
these men tell the truth or were they trying to present positive faces
of themselves to me and to the potential audience of the study?"[16] I
am less concerned about the issue in the case of the military officers (who
struck me as quite bold, frank, and forthright); and OMB specialists, who
were chiefly concerned with economic problems and program evaluation
in domestic affairs, would have little reason not to be candid. But diplomats are skilled at the gracious manipulation of their self-presentation and
might be centrally concerned with putting forward a positive face.

In general I am inclined to believe that those who responded did so candidly. The questionnaire was completed anonymously, did not deal with unusually sensitive issues, and the research was independent, done in association with a respected university, and had no official connection with bureaucratic superiors. Those who might feel pressured to alter responses had the far easier course of simply dropping the questionnaire into a wastebasket. Moreover each man could request, through a separate form, a report on the results of the study—the number returning the form was approximately equal to the number returning the questionnaire. Thus there was a minor incentive to be candid (i.e., the production of an accurate report), and I suspect fewer would have requested such a report if they felt they were providing biased data.

The strongest test for validity is whether the data obtained are internally consistent and converge with other data from other sources. The plausible interscale correlations reported in chapter 3 suggest either honesty or enormous and laborious systematic falsification; the first alternative seems far more likely. Compared with my expectations and prior knowledge I found no surprises, although there probably should be some adjustments, as discussed earlier in this appendix. The general portrait— well-educated, high self-esteem men, a basic assumption of the personal trustworthiness of others, at least moderately high ambition, a tendency toward competition, relative freedom from obvious neurotic symptoms— was what one would plausibly expect to find in the professional government elite of an advanced industrial country where both entrance and promotion are on the basis of merit. The picture may be slanted a bit toward the positive side but not, I think, excessively.

The only slight surprises encountered were on the policy side. Extrapolating from myself (as I conclude these men do as well), I was surprised to find as high a degree of tendency to use military force and to be fearful of Soviet ambitions as were reported by diplomats. I would also have expected efforts to present a "positive" face in the waning days of American involvement in Vietnam to have produced a low percentage of people who said they favored that war. But such a self-portrayal did not appear (almost two-thirds of diplomatic respondents and 83% of military officers said they would have favored an American war in Vietnam if they believed it would have succeeded by the end of 1968). Since my prior expectations

were not based on hard data, I am inclined to accept as reasonably valid
the responses obtained here, with the reservations, expressed above, that
some *increase* in the tendency to use force, in international mistrust, and
in the fear of the Soviet Union should be made if the reader wishes to extrapolate from the sample to the State Department as a whole.

Good evidence for the validity of responses is the coherent pattern of
correlations in the data that correspond with theoretical expectations. And
these results, which show self-expressive generalization, mesh closely with
the similar results obtained independently with the historical data of actual
decisions between 1898 and 1968.[17]

One further question is whether the attitude responses given on the
paper-and-pencil questionnaire employed here will predict to actual policy
preferences in real world situations.[18] This general question can be decomposed into two subsidiary questions. First, will any of the attitude scales
predict simply and directly to behavior? The answer is "probably not." In
my view a field-theory orientation, a view of behavior as the result of *multiple* forces, considerations, and attitudes, is most appropriate for thinking
about foreign policy behavior. A single predisposition is one, but only one,
significant component. Second, do the attitude scales used efficiently represent such a significant component of the determinants of behavior in
actual situations? This question cannot in the end be answered by paper-
and-pencil tests, and this was one reason for the coordinate historical study,
which found that dominance over subordinates, a trait associated with
ambition, did indeed predict the use of force. But there are plausible
reasons to think the answers reported do have substantial validity, especially
for diplomats and probably for the military officers. These were well-
educated and sophisticated professionals with considerable practice and
experience (typically 15–20 years of career service) in facing the kinds of
issues that were presented here, men working in an environment in which
such issues are discussed both professionally and socially. Moreover the
questions posed in the questionnaire were cast in terms of concrete policy
situations and specific issues, close to real issues, and presented with "hard
phrasing" rather than general beliefs or sloganistic sentiments (e.g., "A
nation faced with a bunch of really dangerous enemies might be better off
to shoot first and ask questions afterward.")[19] The attitudes of these men

were assessed by asking them fairly directly about their actual views developed and manifested in real-world situations.

The usual worry is that paper-and-pencil tests will be taken to predict more strongly to future behavior than is warranted. But, especially given the high percentage of cases explained by the personality trait of dominance over subordinates in the historical study, an opposite (and perhaps more relevant) validity question arises; namely, whether paper-and-pencil correlations obtained during a relatively tranquil period in international relations may *understate* seriously the effect of personality engagement on policy decisions in real-world decisions. It may be that emotional arousal and actually making decisions personally (often in a crisis atmosphere) decrease higher cognitive functioning and engage personal emotional dynamics with *greater* force than is captured fully by asking men sitting calmly at their desks, somewhat psychologically removed from these situations, what they would do.[20]

Validity of Results—Correction for Attenuation and the Conservatism of Results

The results reported in chapters 4 and 5 probably underestimate the impact of variations in personality on variations in policy and perception. Although a rigorous mathematical treatment is complex, a brief prose sketch of the problems of measurement error and of "attenuation" can outline the source of the underestimation.[21] It is generally known that a man's answer to questions tends to vary somewhat over even short periods of time (at least for the kinds of questions used in personality and attitude scales). The traditional theory of psychological measurement assumes that, if one is measuring an enduring personality trait or a meaningful attitude, then each individual can be thought to have one "true" score on the scale which is employed. The variability of the "observed" score from one testing to the next is conceptualized as "measurement error." (The mean of a man's observed scores across repeated tests is his true score; error terms are assumed to be normally distributed about the mean and to be uncorrelated with the true score.)

The reader will have noted that many of the relationships which have

been reported have a low R^2. In other words, variation in any one personality factor accounts, by itself, for only a small proportion of the variation
in policy views. And, while I expect this is correct, the R^2 values which are
reported could be biased downward substantially by the presence of measurement error of the type described. If we assume that the scales used in
the study have a test-retest correlation of .75 (a reasonable assumption for
scales of this type and length), then (in a bivariate regression) the R^2 value
should be adjusted upwards by 7/9. The upward adjustment of R^2 tells us
the proportion of variance in the dependent variable which we have explained out of the total variance we *could* explain. (The adjustment has
the effect of subtracting from the observed variation an estimate of the
amount of that variation due simply to measurement error).

As just illustrated, regression results are quite sensitive to measurement
error. Not only is the computed R^2 biased toward zero, but the b coefficient also tends toward zero (and, in the hypothetical example above it
should be increased by one third in absolute value), other estimates of error
become too large, the computed t and F values are too low, and so forth.

I have not applied these corrections for attenuation to my results. In
part this is because the rationales for such corrections are generally un-
familiar and employing them might make my argument appear self-serving
and suspicious. In part it is because the n-dimensional mathematics involved
in adjustment is complex and would not alter the conclusions I draw. The
crucial point, however, is that measurement difficulties of the type I have
described do not affect results in unknown ways. They *always* tend, in the
bivariate case, to make the reported results an *underestimate* of the significance and strength of impact of the variables being tested, and thus the
case for the conclusions is stronger than is apparent on the surface.

Appendix B
Statistical Tables for the State
Department Study

Table B.1

Advocacy of Use of Force (Percent of Cases) as Determined by Selected
Personality Traits

	a_0	OMB Intercept Shift	NWC Intercept Shift	Personality Trait
1	30.05	—	—	2.595 Hostility (2.04)
2	30.3	—	19.7 (4.9)***	10.9 Competitiveness (4.2)***
3	17.3	—	—	3.4 Ideal Self Activity-power (1.8)*
4	43.1	−80.5 (24.7)***	20.2 (4.3)***	0 Idealization of American Foreign Policy
5	19.6	—	—	.9 Neuroticism (.3)**
6	43.1	−10.1 (4.8)*	11.5 (5.9)*	0 Neuroticism
7	55.3	−9.5 (4.8)*	20.1 (4.3)***	−1.6 Trust (.51)**
8	96	—	−200.3 (47.1)***	−5.5 Self-esteem (2.5)*
9	79	—	18.1 (4.3)***	−6.1 Political Transcendence (2.3)**

*$p(t) < .05$ **$p(t) < 01$ ***$p(t) < .001$

The equation from entry 2 predicts to scenarios involving underdeveloped countries
only; the equation from entry 5 predicts to deviations from overall mean.

OMB Slope Shift	NWC Slope Shift	R^2	F
−2.09 (.94)**	3.70 (.82)***	.14	$F(3,213) = 11.7$ $p(F) < 5 \times 10^{-7}$
−15.15 (6.66)**	—	.15	$F(3,214) = 12.9$ $p(F) < 1 \times 10^{-8}$
−1.33 (.64)*	2.3 (.5)***	.15	$F(3,214) = 12.7$ $p(F) < 2 \times 10^{-7}$
9.7 (3.4)***	— —	.16	$F(3,210) = 13.8$ $p(F) < 4 \times 10^{-8}$
—	—	.03	$F(1,225) = 7.2$ $p(F) < .009$
—	2.71 (1.3)*	.15	$F(3,214) = 12.4$ $p(F) < 2 \times 10^{-7}$
—	—	.16	$F(3,213) = 14.4$ $p(F) < 2 \times 10^{-8}$
−1.8 (.57)**	25.7 (5.5)***	.22	$F(4,199) = 14$ $p(F) < 5 \times 10^{-10}$
−1.3 (0.8)	—	.16	$F(3,213) = 14$ $p(F) < 3 \times 10^{-8}$

Table B.2
Desired Military Capability (Number of Wars) as Determined by Selected Personality Traits

	a_O	OMB Intercept Shift	NWC Intercept Shift	Personality Trait
1	1.43	—	—	0 Hostility
2	1.43	—	—	0 Competitiveness
3	1.47	—	.17 (.08)*	0 Dominance
4	1.61	—	.67 (.07)***	−.068 Trust (.05)
5	.26	—	4.6 (.79)***	.124 Self-esteem (.04)**
6	2.11	—	.16 (.08)*	−.11 Political transcendence (.04)**

*$p(t) < .05$ **$p(t) < .01$ ***$p(t) < .001$

OMB Slope Shift	NWC Slope Shift	R^2	F
—	.04 (.01)**	.04	$F(1,199) = 7.6$ $p(F) < .007$
—	.23 (.08)**	.04	$F(1,199) = 8.1$ $p(F) < .006$
−.32 (.15)*	—	.06	$F(2,198) = 5.9$ $p(F) < .004$
−.07 (.05)	—	.09	$F(3,197) = 6.2$ $p(F) < .0005$
—	−.51 (.09)***	.17	$F(3,197) = 13$ $p(F) < 7 \times 10^{-8}$
—	—	.07	$F(2,198) = 7.8$ $p(F) < 6 \times 10^{-4}$

Table B.3

Perceptions of Soviet Foreign Policy as Determined by Selected Personality Traits

	a_O	Personality Trait	R^2	F
A. Activity-Power				
1	6.09	.164 Self: Activity-power (.04)**	.05	$F(1,199) = 10.5$ $p(F) < .002$
2	5.10	.27 Ideal self: Activity-power (.07)**	.07	$F(1,216) = 16.9$ $p(F) < .0002$
3	5.69	.267 Dominance (.09)**	.04	$F(1,216) = 8.6$ $p(F) < .004$
B. Menace				
1	3.65	.403 Ideal self: Activity-power (.148)**	.03	$F(1,217) = 7.4$ $p(F) < .007$
2	4.41	.423 Dominance (.204)*	.02	$F(1,216) = 4.3$ $p(F) < .04$
3	6.29	.79 Competitiveness (.31)*	.03	$F(1,216) = 6.6$ $p(F) < .02$
4	7.55	−.21 Neuroticism (.05)***	.07	$F(1,216) = 16.1$ $p(F) < 4 \times 10^{-5}$

$*p < .05$ $**p < .01$ $***p < .001$

No intercept shift or slope shift terms entered the best-fit equations.

Appendix C
The Possibility of Personal Bias

Much of what passes for knowledge at any given time is likely to be more or less mistaken.

Bertrand Russell

The disillusioning image of American foreign policy decision making—and of the history of American foreign policy since 1898—proposed by this book is critical of the masked error-prone subjectivism and overconfidence in judgments about reality involved in major decisions. I think it is appropriate, then, to consider here whether there may be similar subjective distortion to my own conclusions and whether they are trustworthy.

With respect to the main conclusions I think the possibility I have distorted reality by personal bias is small. The evidence has been assembled by explicit indicators and the conclusions drawn by explicit and formal methods: neither I nor the reader has to depend on any bold rhetoric or mystical claims to omniscience on my part. Moreover the main conclusions are supported by four reinforcing tiers of hard evidence: (1) extensive cross-cultural work by anthropologists which shows the war propensity of a society to depend partly on whether its people are competitive and ambitious; (2) mass public opinion surveys in the United States and foreign countries previously conducted by other social scientists, which find similar personality effects. The two original studies reported in this volume, the State Department study (3) and the historical study (4), add to this base with direct evidence that part of the modal personality of American elites has a central effect on the decision to use force among both professional specialists and presidents and secretaries of state. Moreover, the image of American elite political behavior built upon these four tiers of evidence is consistent with the large ancillary body of literature from psychology on the generalization of private motives and overconfident perception in the partially ambiguous situations of projective tests. Both the formal methods of the two original studies reported here and their strong convergence with the conclusions of many independent researchers give me confidence that the image I propose goes beyond mere plausible conjecture, is worthy of public attention, and indeed has a substantially greater claim to scientific merit than the trust that political leaders typically decide the fates of others on judgments of war and the use of force "rationally, in the public's interest."

But there are two instances in which there are personal elements shaping the text. First, this study had considerable emotional charge for me. I was at times horrified and angered that, although the warning was sounded by Lasswell forty years ago, the world's political leaders were never responsible, professional, or self-critical enough to undertake this kind of investigation themselves. I suspect a lot of people have died unnecessarily because of avoidable mistakes over the subsequent years: the hands of ignorance drip blood. I have been as fair and sympathetic as I can in the text, but I feel greater sympathy for victims than for elites, and there are limits to how completely sympathetic I feel about leaders with power and responsibility who have made others victims of their own failures.

Second, I may misunderstand the power of competitiveness and personal ambition on pronouncements about reality and on policy. In writing this book I have implicitly imagined that politicians today might be basically sincere professionals of great personal integrity who will now investigate, question, and disengage the automatic linkages of their competition and ambition to fear and war once they directly see the evidence and the problem in perspective. But perhaps I am naive about this: some of my colleagues and graduate students find more plausible than I do both the argument that men in power like too much their ego trips of self-expression and personalism, and the argument that ambitious and competitive people will continue to adopt scare rhetoric and advocate force because this brings them prominence, votes, or career advancement. I hope that I am right and these cynical views of human nature are wrong: time will tell.

Notes and References

Chapter 1

1. A synthesis of research on the decision is Irving L. Janis, *Victims of Groupthink: A Psychological Study of Foreign Policy Decisions and Fiascoes* (Boston: Houghton Mifflin, 1972). Insider accounts include Arthur Schlesinger, Jr., *A Thousand Days* (Boston: Houghton Mifflin, 1965): Theodore Sorenson, *Kennedy* (New York: Bantam edition, 1966); Roger Hilsman, *To Move a Nation* (New York: Doubleday, 1967).

2. David Halberstam, *The Best and the Brightest* (New York: Random House, 1972).

3. An extended account of the invasion is K. E. Meyer and T. Szulc, *The Cuban Invasion* (New York: Praeger, 1962).

4. See Karl W. Deutsch and Dieter Senghaas, "The Steps to War: A Survey of System Levels, Decision Stages, and Research Results" in Patrick J. McGowan (ed.) *Sage International Yearbook of Foreign Policy Studies,* vol. 1 (Beverly Hills: Sage Publications, 1973), pp. 275–329, p. 300.

5. Janis (see n. 1); Alexander L. George, "The Case for Multiple Advocacy in Making Foreign Policy," *American Political Science Review,* LXVI (Sept., 1972), pp. 751–785. See also the comment by I. M. Destler and the rejoinder by George, ibid., pp. 786–795.

6. For example, Harold D. Lasswell, *Power and Personality* (New York: Norton, 1948) and *Psychopathology and Politics* (Chicago: University of Chicago Press, 1930); James D. Barber, *The Lawmakers* (New Haven: Yale University Press, 1965) and *The Presidential Character* (Englewood Cliffs: Prentice Hall, 1972); Glendon Schubert, *Quantitative Analysis of Judicial Behavior* (Glencoe, Illinois: The Free Press, 1959); Arnold Rogow, *James Forrestal: A Study of Personality, Politics, and Policy* (New York: Macmillan, 1963); Alexander and Juliette George, *Woodrow Wilson and Colonel House: A Personality Study* (New York: Dover paperback, 1964); Ole Holsti, "Cognitive Dynamics and Images of the Enemy: Dulles and Russia" in David Finlay et al., *Enemies in Politics* (Chicago: Rand McNally, 1967), pp. 25–96; and "The 'Operational Code' Approach to the Study of Political Leaders: John Foster Dulles' Philosophical and Instrumental Beliefs," *Canadian Journal of Political Science,* III:1 (March, 1970), pp. 123–157; Betty Glad, *Charles Evans Hughes and the Illusions of Innocence* (Urbana: University of Illinois Press, 1966); Margaret Hermann, "How Leaders Process Information and the Effect on Foreign Policy, An Exploratory Study", in James N. Rosenau (ed.), *Comparing Foreign Policies: Theories, Finding, and Methods* (Beverly Hills: Sage, 1974); John Toland, *Adolph Hitler* (New York: Doubleday, 1976); Erik Erikson, *Young Man Luther* (New York: Norton, 1958) and *Gandhi's Truth* (New York: Norton, 1969); Bruce Mazlish, *In Search of Nixon* (New York: Basic Books. 1972); Bruce Mazlish, *The Revolutionary Ascetic: Evolution of a Political Type* (New York: Basic Books, 1976); Bruce Mazlish, *Kissinger: The European Mind in American Politics* (New York: Basic Books, 1976); Lucian Pye, *Mao Tse Tung: The Man in the Leader* (New York: Basic Books, 1976); Doris Kearns, *Lyndon Johnson and the American Dream* (New York: Harper and Row, 1976); Nancy Clinch, *The Kennedy Neurosis* (New York: Grosset and Dunlop, 1973); Robert

Tucker, *Stalin as Revolutionary 1879-1929* (New York: Norton, 1974); Robert Tucker, "The Georges' Wilson Reexamined: An Essay on Psychobiography." *American Political Science Review,* 71:2 (June, 1977), pp. 606-618; Irving Lefberg, *Analyzing Judicial Change: the Uses of Systematic Biography* (unpublished doctoral thesis in progress, M.I.T.); Walter C. Langer, *The Mind of Adolph Hitler* (New York: Basic Books, 1972).

7. Schlesinger (n. 1); Janis (n. 1).

8. Guerilla warfare was a preoccupation of Kennedy even when he was in the Senate. See Schlesinger (n. 1), pp. 340-342.

9. Schlesinger (n. 1).

Chapter 2

1. See Quincy Wright, *A Study of War* (Chicago: University of Chicago Press, 1964), abridged edition, pp. 319-322. Related studies of the way wars are justified are Kjell Goldmann, *International Norms and War Between States* (Stockholm: Laromedelsforlagen, 1971) and F. M. Kail, *What Washington Said: Administration Rhetoric and the Vietnam War* (New York: Harper and Row, 1973).

2. A classic article in the debate is Sidney Verba, "Assumptions of Rationality and Non-Rationality in Models of the International System," in Klaus Knorr and Sidney Verba (eds.), *The International System: Theoretical Essays* (Princeton: Princeton University Press, 1961), pp. 93-117. The most recent review of the issues is Ole Holsti, "Foreign Policy Formation Viewed Cognitively" in Robert M. Axelrod (ed.), *Structure of Decision: The Cognitive Maps of Political Elites* (Princeton: Princeton University Press, 1976), pp. 18-54. See also Morton Kaplan, *On Historical and Political Knowing* (Chicago: University of Chicago Press, 1972). pp. 109-121.

3. General reviews of psychological approaches to international relations include Herbert Kelman and Alfred Bloom, "Assumptive Frameworks in International Politics" in Jeanne Knutson (ed.), *Handbook of Political Psychology* (San Franscisco: Jossey-Bass, 1973), pp. 261-295; Amitai Etzioni, "Social Psychological Aspects of International Relations" in G. Lindzey and G. Aronson (eds.), *The Handbook of Social Psychology* second edition (Reading, Mass.: Addison-Wesley, 1969), vol. 5, pp. 538-601; James C. Davies, "Aggression, Violence, Revolution, and War" in Jeanne Knutson (ed.), *Handbook of Political Psychology* (San Francisco: Jossey-Bass, 1973), pp. 234-260. Broad overviews of international relations theory are James E. Dougherty and Robert Pfaltzgraff, Jr., *Contending Theories of International Relations* (Philadelphia: Lippincott, 1971) and Kenneth N. Waltz, "Theory of International Relations," in Fred I. Greenstein and Nelson Polsby (eds.), *Handbook of Political Science* (Reading, Mass.: Addison-Wesley, 1975), vol. 8, pp. 1-85.

On the role of the individual decision maker see Holsti (n. 2); Herbert Kelman, "The Role of the Individual in International Relations: Some Conceptual and Methodological Considerations," *Journal of International Affairs,* 24:1 (1970), pp. 1-17; Lloyd Jensen, "Foreign Policy Calculation" in Michael Haas (ed.), *International Sys-*

tems: A Behavioral Approach (New York: Chandler, 1974), pp. 77–97; Samuel A. Kirkpatrick, "Psychological Views of Decision-Making" in Cornelius P. Cotter (ed.), *Political Science Annual: Individual Decision Making* (Indianapolis: Bobbs-Merrill, 1975); Anthony A. D'Amato, "Psychological Constructs in Foreign Policy Prediction," *Journal of Conflict Resolution* 11 (1967), pp. 294–311; John D. Steinbruner, *The Cybernetic Theory of Decision* (Princeton: Princeton University Press, 1974), ch. 4; Margaret Hermann, "Effect of Personal Characteristics of Leaders on Foreign Policy" in M. A. East et al. (eds.), *Why Nations Act* (Beverly Hills: Sage, 1977).

Of special methodological importance are Fred I. Greenstein's *Personality and Politics: Problems of Evidence, Inference, and Conceptualization* (Chicago: Markham, 1969), and (treating personality experimentally) Donald T. Campbell, "Reforms as Experiments" in James Caporaso and Leslie Roos, Jr. (eds.), *Quasi-Experimental Approaches* (Evanston: Northwestern University Press, 1973).

4. For a more elaborate schema see M. Brewster Smith, "A Map for the Analysis of Personality and Politics," reprinted in Fred I. Greenstein and Michael Lerner (eds.), *A Source Book for the Analysis of Personality and Politics* (Chicago: Markham, 1971), pp. 34–44. A related approach is Lloyd Etheredge, *The Case of the Unreturned Cafeteria Trays* (Washington: American Political Science Association, 1976).

5. Frances Fitzgerald, *Fire in the Lake: The Vietnamese and the Americans in Vietnam* (New York: Random House, 1972), ch. 1 et passim.

6. A remarkably thorough study based on over a decade's research is Robert Jervis, *Perception and Misperception in International Relations* (Princeton: Princeton University Press, 1976). See also Axelrod (n. 2), and Steinbruner (n. 3), ch. 4.

7. For a review see Holsti (n. 2); the key original article in the operational code approach is Alexander L. George, "The Operational Code: A Neglected Approach to the Study of Political Leaders and Decision Making," *International Studies Quarterly*, 13 (1969), pp. 109–222.

If I understand the George-Holsti position correctly it is that emotional dynamics usually become operative through, and can be captured by a study of, cognitive processes embodied in the structure of an operational code.

8. See Ole Holsti and Alexander L. George, "The Effects of Stress on the Performance of Foreign Policy-Makers" in C. P. Cotter (ed.), *Political Science Annual: Individual Decision-Making* (Indianapolis: Bobbs-Merrill, 1975); Alexander L. George, "Adaptation to Stress in Political Decision Making: the Individual, Small Group, and Organizational Contexts" in G. V. Coelho et al. (eds.), *Coping and Adaptation* (New York: Basic Books, 1974); Irving Janis and Leon Mann, *Decision Making: A Psychological Analysis of Conflict, Choice and Commitment* (New York: Free Press, 1977).

Work on aggressive drives is ably reviewed by Stephen Nelson, "Nature/Nurture Revisited I: A Review of the Biological Bases of Conflict," *Journal of Conflict Resolution*, 18 (1974), pp. 285–335, and in Davies (n. 3).

Crisis decision making is addressed in Charles F. Hermann (ed.), *International Crisis: Insights from Behavioral Science* (New York: Free Press, 1972).

Work related to "national character" determinants of national war-likeness include Quincy Wright (n. 1); Philip Slater, *Footholds* (New York: Dutton, 1977) chs. 9, 10 and apps. A, B; Philip Slater, *The Glory of Hera* (Boston: Beacon Press, 1971); David Levinson, "What Have We Learned from Cross-Cultural Surveys?" *American Behavioral Scientist,* 20:5 (May-June, 1977), pp. 757–792; David McClelland, *Power: the Inner Experience* (New York: Irvington, 1975).

9. Among the most wide-ranging studies are Margaret Hermann, "How Leaders Process Information and the Effect in Foreign Policy: An Exploratory Study" in James N. Rosenau (ed.), *Comparing Foreign Policies, Theories, Findings, and Methods* (Beverly Hills: Sage, 1974); see the works cited in note 6 of chapter 1 of the present book; Holsti (n. 2), overlaps with emotional dynamic categories.

A useful additional reference is John Raser, "Personal Characteristics of Political Decision-Makers: A Literature Review," *Papers of the Peace Research Society (International),* 5 (1966), pp. 161–181. Comparative data on American presidents' motivational patterns and wars in David Winter, *The Power Motive* (New York: Free Press, 1973), have also been a useful contribution.

10. Irving L. Janis, *Victims of Groupthink: A Psychological Study of Foreign Policy Decisions and Fiascoes* (Boston: Houghton Mifflin, 1972); Janis and Mann (n. 8); Joseph DeRivera, *The Psychological Dimension of Foreign Policy* (Columbus: Merrill, 1968) is an important contribution to this topic of group processes as well as more generally.

11. Chris Argyris, *Some Causes of Organizational Ineffectiveness Within the Department of State,* Occasional Paper No. 2 of the Center for International Systems Research (Washington: Department of State, 1967).

12. A review is Holsti (n. 2). Basic references are Graham T. Allison, *Essence of Decision: Explaining the Cuban Missile Crisis* (Boston: Little, Brown, 1971); Morton Halperin, *Bureaucratic Politics and Foreign Policy* (Washington, DC: Brookings Institution, 1974).

13. I am here following Gergen in being skeptical of the possibility of deriving cross-contextual fixed coefficients. See Kenneth Gergen, "Social Psychology as History," *Journal of Personality and Social Psychology,* 26:2 (1973), pp. 309–320.

14. Bjorn Christiansen, *Attitudes Towards Foreign Affairs as a Function of Personality* (Oslo: Oslo University Press, 1959). General reviews of the personality–foreign policy literature may be found in Christiansen, Tom Atkinson, *A Propositional Inventory of Empirical Work Involving Foreign Affairs and National Security Attitudes, 1960–1966* (Oak Ridge: Oak Ridge National Laboratory, 1967); Kenneth W. Terhune, "The Effects of Personality in Cooperation and Conflict" in Paul Swingle (ed.), *The Structure of Conflict* (New York: Academic Press, 1970), pp. 193–204; William Eckhardt and Theo. Lentz, "Factors of War/Peace Attitudes" *Peace Research Reviews,* I:5 (October, 1967), entire; Herbert McClosky, "Personality and Attitude Correlates of Foreign Policy Orientation" in James N. Rosenau (ed.), *Domestic Sources of Foreign Policy* (New York: Free Press, 1967), pp. 51–109; Paul Sniderman and Jack Cit-

rin, "Psychological Sources of Political Belief: Self-Esteem and Isolationist Attitudes," *American Political Science Review,* LXV:2 (June, 1971), pp. 401–417; William Eckhardt, "Ideology and Personality in Social Attitudes," *Peace Research Reviews,* III:2 (April, 1969), entire; William Eckhardt and N. Alcock, "Ideology and
Personality in War/Peace Attitudes," *Journal of Social Psychology,* 81 (1970), pp.
105–116; William Eckhardt, "The Military-Industrial Personality," *Journal of Contemporary Revolutions,* 3:4 (1971), pp. 74–87; Slater (n. 8).

15. Christiansen (n. 14).

16. Eckhardt, "Ideology and Personality in Social Attitudes" (n. 14).

17. These could be construed as values, although I think such fantasies are less cere-
bral and more visceral than the term "values" implies. For evidence of generalization
of values see William Scott, "International Ideology and Interpersonal Ideology,"
Public Opinion Quarterly, 24 (1960), pp. 419–435.

18. William Graham Sumner, *Folkways* (New York: Ginn, 1906).

19. Cited in Robert A. LeVine and Donald T. Campbell, *Ethnocentrism: Theories of
Conflict, Ethnic Attitudes, and Group Behavior* (New York: Wiley 1972), p. 213.

20. LeVine and Campbell, ibid., provide a systematic review of evidence and alternative formulations.

21. See Fitzgerald (n. 5).

22. See Eckhardt and Lentz (n. 14); McClosky (n. 14); Sniderman and Citrin (n. 14).

23. McClosky (n. 14), pp. 106–107.

24. David C. Garnham, "Attitude and Personality Patterns of United States Foreign
Service Officers," *American Journal of Political Science* 18:3 (1974), pp. 31–39;
Bernard Mennis, *American Foreign Policy Officials: Who They Are and What They
Believe Regarding International Politics* (Columbus: Ohio State University Press,
1971). For additional data on FSO attitude correlates see Andrew Semmel, "Some
Correlates of Foreign Policy Attitudes among Foreign Service Officers" (unpublished
doctoral thesis, University of Michigan, Ann Arbor, 1972).

25. Lloyd Etheredge, *Political Psychology and Qualitative Metaphysics* (unpublished
manuscript); "Hardball Politics: A Model" (forthcoming); and "Hypnosis and Order"
in John Sweeney (ed.), *Politics and Psychology* (tentative title, forthcoming).

26. Cited on frontispiece of Oscar Jaszi, *The Dissolution of Hapsburg Monarchy*
(Chicago: University of Chicago Press, 1929); paperback edition, 1961.

27. Henry A. Kissinger, "Domestic Structure and Foreign Policy," *Daedalus,* XCV
(Spring, 1966), pp. 503–529. It should be noted that Kissinger based his analysis at
the group level and implied that mistrust would be a realistic lesson for these men to
learn from past experiences; such mistrust could be qualitatively different (in origin,
intensity, and psychological consequences) from that which might arise between individuals in the United States.

28. Argyris (n. 11).

29. Verba (n. 2).

30. James D. Barber, *Power in Committees: An Experiment in the Governmental Process* (Chicago: Rand McNally, 1966), pp. 75–82.

31. Robert E. Lane, *Political Ideology; Why the American Common Man Believes What He Does* (Glencoe: Free Press, 1962), p. 468. Lane expands this thesis in his study of personality and belief systems among underclassmen at Adams College: "The aggressive man sees the government as aggressive . . . Here we have men . . . generalizing their need to be liked so that government officials are seen to be in the grip of this same need . . ." Robert E. Lane, *Political Thinking and Consciousness: The Private Life of the Political Mind* (Chicago: Markham, 1969), p. 141.

32. Cited in Mennis (n. 24), p. 173.

33. See LeVine and Campbell (n. 19) for a general review. This is a plausible albeit a rather crude operationalization since what is repressed may not be the direct opposite of what is manifest in interpersonal relations. It is conceivable that projection of unconscious elements of personality are represented in the intercept term of the equation for the dependent variable in chapter 5 of the present work with variations in manifest personal dynamics affecting only variations from this intercept.

Chapter 3

1. Full documentation and extensive statistical appendices for these items and others not discussed in this manuscript are available in the thesis version: Lloyd S. Etheredge, *A World of Men: The Private Sources of American Foreign Policy* (unpublished doctoral thesis, Yale University, 1974) available through University Microfilms. Appendix A of the present book discusses the possible sensitivity of conclusions to sampling bias and other issues.

2. These numbers reflect a 78% response from 50 people contacted at OMB and 49% of the 100 military officers in the resident class at NWC.

3. I will refer to "men" throughout since 98% of FSOs, 87% of OMB respondents, and all military officers were male. The number of women was too small to permit separate statistical analysis.

4. Separate analysis by length of total service abroad, length of service in underdeveloped countries, and length of service in Communist bloc countries failed to identify any consistent effects from these experiences on the variables in the study.

5. This represents, according to informants, a typical pattern at OMB, where young men and women work at the agency for 3–7 years and then move out to a substantive job in another government agency. Some respondents at OMB were there as a career and were in their 50s. The foreign service and military are career services.

6. Reprinted in John Robinson and Philip Shaver, *Measures of Social Psychological Attitudes* (Ann Arbor: Survey Research Center, 1969), pp. 135–139. On convergent

and discriminant validity see David L. Hamilton, "The Comparative Study of Five Methods of Assessing Self-Esteem, Dominance, and Dogmatism," *Educational and Psychological Measurement,* 31 (Summer, 1971), pp. 441–452. On the ICL weighting system see Rolfe LaForge et al., "The Interpersonal Dimension of Personality: II. An Objective Study of Repression," *Journal of Personality,* 23:1 (September, 1954), pp. 129–153.

7. For example over two thirds of men in all groups checked "independent," "likes responsibility," "makes a good impression," and "friendly" while less than 10% checked "easily led," "meek," or "cold and unfeeling." These are of course *self*-ratings, and the ICL scoring system controls for social desirability response set (i.e., the tendency to give good-sounding but untrue responses).

8. Independence has also been reported for FSO's by Walther in his study for the Herter Commission. Walther compared FSOs with other occupational groups and found that "... the Foreign Service Officer tends to score high on the Self-confidence, Academic Data, Problem Analysis, Resourceful Accomplishment . . . Persuasive Leadership, and Autonomous scales. These results suggest that he likes work that combines interpreting data and influencing other people . . . his preferred style for working with a formal organization is to do the work himself rather than to work through a hierarchy. They greatly value personal intellectual achievement . . ." Regis Walther, *Orientations and Behavioral Styles of Foreign Service Officers* (New York: Carnegie Endowment for International Peace, 1965), p. 16.

9. "Forceful" was checked by 58.9% of FSOs, 21.6% at OMB, and 67.3% of military officers; p (OMB–FSO) ns, p (FSO–NWC) $< .001$, p (OMB–NWC) $< 7 \times 10^{-5}$. "Stern but fair" percentages were 25.4% (FSO), 29.7% (OMB), 51.0% (NWC): p (FSO–NWC) $< .002$, others ns. "Very respectful to authority" percentages were 31.0% (FSO), 35.1% (OMB), 65.3% (NWC); p (OMB–FSO) ns, p (FSO–NWC) $< 7 \times 10^{-5}$, p (OMB–FSO) $< .01$. Significance levels determined by χ^2 with Yates correction.

The Leary scoring system "nets" dominance and submission to obtain an overall score, a methodological shortcoming with a military group. Decomposed dominance and submission scores are suspect because the "net score" weighting procedure controls for social desirability response set. All groups were slightly more dominant and affectionate than the theoretical mean without significant group mean differences in net scores.

10. p (OMB–FSO) ns, p (FSO–NWC) $< 3 \times 10^{-4}$, p (OMB–NWC) $< .04$.

11. 8.92 (FSO), 8.61 (OMB), 8.97 (NWC); p (OMB–FSO) $< .03$, p (FSO–NWC) ns, p (OMB–NWC) $< .05$. Here, and for all other interval scales, statistical significance of differences was assessed by t-test based on an F-test with a $p < .05$ threshold for rejection of the null hypothesis of similar group variances. Significance levels of differences are not simply a product of absolute differences in means but depend as well on variances and number of respondents. For additional detail on the semantic differential adjective scales used here see appendix A, also Charles Osgood et al., *The Measurement of Meaning* (Urbana: University of Illinois Press, 1957), and J. Snider and C. Osgood (eds.), *Semantic Differential Technique: A Sourcebook*

Chicago: Aldine, 1969.) Connotative similarity was determined by factor analysis-varimax criteria and orthogonal rotation, as described in appendix A.

12. An indication of high sense of esteem was an answer to a question on the SRC Strongmindedness scale (not reported in detail). Asked "When you get into an argument do you usually get your own way or do you often give in?" sixty percent of American adults say they "often give in" while only 50% at OMB checked this, 37% at the State, and only 27% at NWC. See the FSOs love of persuading people found by Walther (n. 8) and the evidence for higher dominance of military officers cited earlier.

On the theoretical and methodological issues involved in the concept of self-esteem see Ruth C. Wylie, "The Present Status of Self Theory" in Edgar F. Borgatta and William W. Lambert (eds.), *Handbook of Personality Theory and Research* (Chicago: Rand McNally, 1968), pp. 728–787, and her *The Self Concept* (Lincoln: University of Nebraska Press, 1961).

13. 3.62 (FSO), 4.41 (OMB), 3.20 (NWC). Of the 1,600 subjects in the Eysenck study, 91% completed all items. For government groups combined, $t = 4.9$, $p(t) < 5 \times 10^{-7}$. Analyzed separately there are strongly significant FSO and NWC differences from British adults. The OMB group shows a likely difference ($t = 1.49$, $p(t) < .07$). See p. 58 of thesis version of the present work; H. J. Eysenck, "A Short Questionnaire for the Measurement of Two Dimensions of Personality," *Journal of Applied Psychology,* 42:1 (1958), pp. 14–17.

14. See Bernard Mennis, *American Foreign Policy Officials: Who They Are and What They Believe Regarding International Politics* (Columbus: Ohio State University Press, 1971); David Garnham, *Attitude and Personality Patterns of Foreign Service Officers and the Conduct of American Foreign Affairs* (unpublished doctoral dissertation, University of Minnesota, 1971).

15. 6.77 (FSO), 6.36 (OMB), 7.61 (NWC); p(OMB–FSO) ns, p(FSO–NWC) $< 8 \times 10^{-5}$, p(OMB–NWC) $< 4 \times 10^{-6}$.

16. 7.74 (FSO), 7.45 (OMB), 8.12 (NWC); p(OMB–FSO) ns, p(FSO–NWC) $< .009$, p(OMB–NWC) $< .001$. For increases from self scores, OMB: $t = 4.39$, $p(t) < .001$; FSO: $t = 6.06$, $p(t) < .001$; NWC: $t = 2.49$, $p(t) < .01$.

17. "Many FSOs are ambitious to become an ambassador." John E. Harr, *The Professional Diplomat* (Princeton: Princeton University Press, 1969), p. 207.

It may be important that Harr finds a substantial number of these ambitious diplomats overestimate the probability of career advancement to ambassadorships: many more think they have a good chance than will ever be able to fit in the available slots. Perhaps ambitious men overestimate the probability of success (a trait which may affect their greater willingness to use force), although an alternative interpretation is that the State Department promotes unrealistically high expectations of career success to retain able and ambitious men. Six hundred men felt they had a "good" chance or better when there were only 85 slots (ibid. p. 207). The discrepancy is slightly exaggerated by Harr, however, since there will be turnover in these 85 slots and not all 600 will compete simultaneously.

18. However, the question of trust within American elites is probably more complex than I have been able to paint it. Argyris conducted an intensive investigation of the State Department and concluded, on the basis of extensive encounter group sessions with diplomats at all levels, that there were exceptionally low levels of interpersonal trust throughout the Department. I think Argyris's contrary results can be partially explained as follows: he found that the State Department has strong group norms favoring rationality in interpersonal relations and disdaining the intrusion of emotion. Further, there was an associated norm that one should avoid candor which might lead to direct conflict. The encounter groups he used called, however, for both the expression of feelings and for candor. Thus Argyris's results may indicate that it was the idea of violating group *norms* which generated considerable anxiety and fears of retaliation. By the criteria Argyris employed (the restriction of certain group norms and the imagined risk of punishment for violating norms) most bureaucratic organizations would probably be characterized by low interpersonal trust.

The difference between the results obtained with the present scale and Argyris's conclusion probably depends, then, on different conceptions of trust. My questions asked about the ordinary assumption of goodwill a man might make in the normal course of his everyday work. Argyris's criteria, that there should be no fear of retaliation for candor, are broader and more difficult to meet. Argyris, *Some Causes of Organizational Ineffectiveness Within the Department of State,* Occasional Paper No. 2 of the Center for International Systems Research (Washington: Department of State, 1967).

For the original scale and national sample results see John P. Robinson et al., *Measures of Political Attitudes* (Ann Arbor: Survey Research Center, 1968), pp. 651-652, 662.

19. Competition between political elites may make political leaders less trusting than these government professionals.

20. By t-test on original six-point interval scale p(OMB-FSO) $< .004$, p(FSO-NWC) $< .001$, p(OMB-NWC) $< .001$. Original items were (Incrementalist): "Actually, I've taken life pretty much as it's happened. I've just taken the course that looked most attractive when the time came to make a choice," and (Long Range Planning): "Frankly, I've usually planned out my life pretty far ahead. I've known exactly where I wanted to go, figured out how to get there, and followed through."

21. These differences may reflect, in part, the different capacities of men in career-oriented hierarchical organizations to make long range plans. They have a clearer socially sanctioned definition of what "success" entails.

22. Political transcendence scores (on a scale of 0 to 10) show higher transcendence among civilians than among members of career services, greatest subordination among military officers: 5.89 (FSO), 6.33 (OMB), 5.56 (NWC); p(OMB-FSO) $< .004$, p(FSO-NWC) $< .004$, p(OMB-NWC) $< .001$.

23. Extraversion scores did not differ significantly across groups and showed the mean of these respondents to be slightly greater than that of British adults. See Eysenck (n. 13).

24. p(OMB-FSO) < .05, p(FSO-NWC) < .001, p(OMB-NWC) < .001.

25. 6.78 (FSO), 6.49 (OMB), 7.12 (NWC), differences not significant. On the related activity-power image of Soviet foreign policy (10 = high activity-power) scores were 7.23 (FSO), 6.92 (OMB), 7.29 (NWC), with intergroup differences again not significant.

26. p(OMB-FSO) < .04, p(FSO-NWC) ns, p(OMB-NWC) < .03. A man could check as many major goals as he thought applied: the other options checked by more than 30% of diplomats were "they are seeking to gain control over oil resources vital to Western Europe and Japan" (48% FSO) and "they want to spread Communist ideology among the Arab peoples" (35.2% FSO). Military officers were much more likely to believe control of oil was a Russian motivation (71.4%, p(FSO-NWC) < .009), and they were far less persuaded of ideological motives (12.2%, p(FSO-NWC) < .005). Significance levels determined by χ^2 with Yates correction and Ns of 125 (FSO), 37 (OMB), 49 (NWC).

27. p < .001.

28. Differences ns.

29. FSO-OMB difference (when weighted for intensity) is significant (p < .04); other differences are not.

30. Lester B. Pearson, *Partners in Development: Report of the Commission on International Development* (New York: Praeger, 1969). This result is important because it seems to establish there is no likelihood of substantial increases in assistance: even the sights of men who tend to be liberal in their domestic politics and internationalist in their foreign policies seem well below the 1% level.

31. The data partially confirm a hypothesis by Bruce Russett that those who favor larger amounts of foreign aid place greater importance on the aid. The hypothesis is confirmed for military aid (the correlation between importance and amount is .387, p < .01). There is no support in the case of economic development assistance (r = .083, ns), possibly because of the special nature of the sample (i.e., almost all men in these groups desire more aid rather than less). See Bruce Russett, "Demography, Salience, and Internationalist Behavior," *Public Opinion Quarterly,* 24 (1960), pp. 658-664.

32. Differences ns.

33. Differences ns.

34. All OMB-NWC differences statistically significant at least at p < .001. The OMB dissent on neutral or pro-American foreign policy is statistically significant at p < .001; there is no essential difference on this item between FSO and NWC respondents.

35. All differences p < .01.

36. FSO-OMB difference weighted for intensity p < .04; other differences ns.

37. p(FSO-OMB) $< 7 \times 10^{-5}$, p(FSO-NWC) ns, p(OMB-NWC) $< .002$.

38. p(FSO-OMB) ns., p(FSO-NWC) $< .02$; p(OMB-NWC) $< .003$.

39. p(FSO-OMB) $< .006$, p(FSO-NWC) $< .003$, p(OMB-NWC) ns.

40. 7.28 (FSO), 6.98 (OMB), 7.82 (NWC). p(OMB-FSO) = ns, p(FSO-NWC) $< .002$, p(OMB-NWC) $< .001$. For hypothesis of desired increase probability of error of rejecting null hypothesis $< .001$ (OMB $t = 5.22$, FSO $t = 6.90$, NWC $t = 8.41$). The hypothesis that the military desired increase is greater than the civilian is also confirmed with $t = 2.54$, $p < .05$.

41. See the further discussion of these items in appendix A.

42. Military officer intensity was significantly ($p < .01$) higher, 2.4, probably what one would want of the men who actually do the fighting.

43. p(FSO-OMB) ns, p(FSO-NWC) $< 4 \times 10^{-8}$, p(OMB-NWC) $< 4 \times 10^{-7}$. Original question was "How would you describe your domestic political views?" with answers given on a 7-point Likert scale.

44. The relation between traditional views of the cold war and the image of current Soviet foreign policy menace became statistically significant ($r = .200$, $N = 224$, $p < .01$). This expansion of the data base to include a broader range of variance—more "hawks" from the military, more "doves" from OMB—provides evidence for the conventional wisdom that a "liberal-conservative" dimension of both perception and policy also exists among elites.

45. This point, that we are dealing with both policy preferences and beliefs about reality *simultaneously,* is crucial to emphasize. Some accounts of hawk-dove or liberal-conservative disagreements contend that the differences are primarily over *values.* This is wrong. The differences are deeper, lying in *internally coherent different experiences of reality.* See also references in note 25 of chapter 2.

Chapter 4

1. In this discussion I am following the convention of imagining the dependent (attitude) scores graphed vertically and the independent (personality trait) scores graphed horizontally. See appendix A for more discussion of methods.

2. Appendix A describes in detail the methods used in the State Department study and the issues they raise. A check for nonlinearity showed that linear equations efficiently captured the relationships.

3. Assuming the equation is correctly specified.

4. There is another number which is represented in the tables as a probability estimate for each of the b_i terms. This number, $p(t)$, is analogous to $p(F)$ and is the probability that the observed values of b_i would result from random processes when the true $b_i = 0$.

5. As the methodology appendix A discusses, there are problems with paper-and-pencil questionnaires (called "attenuation") with a result that the b and R^2 values reported here are probably too low and the $p(t)$ and $p(F)$ values too high (i.e., the derived results are even more nonrandom than calculated).

6. This was also true of two additional semantic differential scores for stability and pragmatism discussed in appendix A.

7. The original 7-point scales were converted to a range of 0 to 10 so that 1.5 units on the transformed scale correspond to .9 units on the original scale. With this transformation the American foreign policy evaluation score = 2.24 + .6 (NWC intercept shift) -1.04 (OMB intercept shift) + .54 (self-evaluation score). The $p(t)$s, were $<$ .01, $< 1 \times 10^{-7}$, $< 1 \times 10^{-4}$. R^2 = .21, SE = 1.43, $F(3,218)$ = 18.8, $p(F) < 8 \times 10^{-11}$

The American foreign policy activity-power score = 5.07 $-.8$ (NWC intercept shift) $-.5$ (OMB intercept shift) + .18 (self-activity power score). The $p(t)$s were $< .002$, $< .01$, $< .003$. R^2 = .09, SE = 1.2, $F(3,218)$ = 8.03, $p(F) < 5 \times 10^{-5}$.

See additional discussion in the thesis version, Lloyd Etheredge, *A World of Men*, unpublished doctoral thesis, Yale University, 1974. (Ann Arbor: University Microfilms).

The closeness of mean rating is usually taken as a better measure of identification than b coefficients or R^2 since, among a group of identifiers, there is likely to be small true score variance relative to measurement error variance, thus depressing b and R^2.

See the discussion of attenuation in appendix A.

8. $p(t)$ of the FSO slope coefficient $< .20$. This observed figure needs to be evaluated in the light of the likely attenuation problem discussed in the appendix A; subtracting random measurement variations, the $p(t)$ may be much smaller.

9. G. K. Chesterton, "The Mistake of the Machine," in his *The Wisdom of Father Brown* (Middlesex: Penguin, 1970), pp. 76–91, esp. p. 77.

10. W. R. Kite, *Attributions of Causality as a Function of the Use of Reward and Punishment*. (unpublished doctoral dissertation, Stanford University, 1964); Barry Schlenker and James Tedeschi, "Interpersonal Attraction and the Exercise of Coercive and Reward Power," *Human Relations*, 25:5 (1973), pp. 427–439.

11. C. L. Wheeler and E. F. Carnes, "Relations among Self-Concepts, Ideal Self-Concepts, and Stereotypes of Probable and Ideal Vocational Choices," *Journal of Counseling Psychology*, 15 (1968), pp. 530–535.

The *gap* between how powerful and active a man feels and his ideal self dreams was a poorer predictor than the ideal self dreams themselves. Apparently, then, the dynamic is the content of the dreams themselves and not the relative deprivation or frustration (in the simple sense measured here) a man feels.

12. This variable, interpersonal trust, could also be considered an indicator of ingroup solidarity. If so, then the results go directly counter to the prediction of ethnocentrism theory and are additional evidence that these men are not ethnocentric in ways that are illuminated by examining intra-elite personality differences.

I do not mean that being highly trusting is necessarily an ideal for an individual; it would be a more widely accepted ideal that he make differentiated, realistic assessments of who he could trust, to what extent, and under what conditions. (That everyone be trustworthy so everyone can be realistically trusting is more properly a desirable attribute of a *system*.) The correlations are unidirectional; mistrust does not predict, as did the neurotic symptoms, either to above or below average advocacy of force or desired capability levels.

13. $p(t)$ of the FSO and NWC slope coefficient $< .20$, for the OMB slope shift coefficient, $p(t) < .08$. See appendix A on corrections for attenuation.

14. The correlations are unidirectional; low self-esteem does not predict, as did neurotic symptoms, either to above or below average advocacy of force or desired capability levels.

15. I do not find this explanation as to why high self-esteem military officers want lower capability levels completely satisfactory. It might be that the NWC intercept term, which has multicollinearity with the group membership interaction term, makes the NWC X self-esteem interaction term b coefficient unstable, but in reality the correlation in the NWC sample is $-.282$ ($N = 40, p < .08$), so the sign of the slope of the regression line is not an artifact, although its magnitude may be poorly estimated.

16. I should emphasize that this is not, to my mind, a test of *authoritarianism* as a personality syndrome (the research of Mennis and Garnham cited in chapter 3 of the present work suggests authoritarianism is quite low among these men). Rather it is a test of transcendence of *routine* political socialization, a test of the self having "grown up" politically.

It is important to note, however, that almost all of these men have high self-evaluations. Since the spatial location of American foreign policy was assessed indirectly by its evaluative score the major component of the variance of the political transcendence score is simply the evaluative score for American foreign policy. The observed results can be read either as "political transcendence produces . . ." or as "those who have objections to American foreign policy tend to believe . . .," and the data do not permit ruling out the second interpretation.

17. This is true provided the equations are correctly specified. An argument for considering bs more important than R^2s in analyzing data is Eric A. Hanushek and John E. Jackson, *Statistical Methods for Social Scientists* (New York: Academic Press, 1977), p. 21.

18. This is a rough measure since, with only 5 items, the use of force scale moves in 20% jumps. Here, however, it is treated as a continuous variable.

19. This is a rough measure since, with only 5 steps, the desired war capability scale moves in ½ war jumps. Here, however, it is treated as a continuous variable.

20. In addition we have already seen two other instances of group-based effects: high dominance domestic policy specialists at OMB want to cut defense spending,

and being a military officer seems to produce a shift exclusively toward military intervention as a result of intrapsychic conflict (neurotic symptoms).

21. Cited in Bengt Abrahamsson, *Military Professionalization and Political Power* (Beverly Hills: Sage Publications, 1972), p. 77. Original source is Charles O. Lerche, Jr., "The Professional Officer and Foreign Policy," *Strategic Subjects Handbook* (Fort Leavenworth: US Army Command and General Staff College, 1967), R 1800-1, p. Li-5f.

Chapter 5

1. There is a possibility that what I have measured as ideal-self dreams may include harsh superego *demands* on the self. See note 24 below.

2. These were mean rankings on the adjective scales discussed earlier (e.g., strong-weak, active-passive, dominating-submitting, etc.).

3. Major differences of mean scores (especially on the evaluative and pragmatism dimensions) between the self-image and the Soviet foreign policy image is the ground for concluding that these men do not, in general, identify with Soviet foreign policy. One could, however, make the case that they identify with the power component of Soviet policy.

4. See the discussion of attenuation in appendix A. These are probably underestimates.

5. There is a negative effect of the ideal self: activity-power score on the comparison image of British foreign policy at OMB: British activity-power = $5.48 - .123$ (ideal self: activity-power score), $p(t)$ and $p(F) < 6 \times 10^{-4}$, $F(1, 196) = 12.71$, $R^2 = .06$, SE = 1.35. My guess is that the economists at OMB were reacting primarily to Britain's economic problems and were "putting it down" to the extent they cared about greater personal vitality and power.

6. From the semantic differential.

7. These effects hold when groups are analyzed separately.

8. 46.3% of the 121 men scoring low on the experience of their own activity and power ($\leqslant 7$) believe the menacing scenario, compared with 66.0% of the 106 scoring above 7. $N = 227$, $\chi^2 = 8.15$, $p(\chi^2) < .005$. χ^2 with Yates correction.

9. 45.5% of the 123 men scoring low on wishes to feel active and powerful ($\leqslant 7.8$) believe the menacing scenario compared with 67% of the 103 scoring above 7.8. $N = 226$, $\chi^2 = 9.6$ $p(\chi^2) < .002$. χ^2 with Yates correction.

10. 48.7% of the 117 men who were incrementalists ($\leqslant 5$) believe the menacing scenario compared with 62.5% of the 107 men who were long range planners. $N = 224$, $\chi^2 = 3.8$, $p(\chi^2) < .05$. χ^2 with Yates correction.

11. 85.3% of the 75 men who were incrementalists believe the traditional version ($\leqslant 5$) compared with 97.0% of the 66 men who were long range planners. $N = 141$,

$\chi^2 = 4.4\ p(\chi^2) < .04.\ \chi^2$ with Yates correction. Only one military officer was a revisionist, too small a number for a statistical test.

12. Evaluation score of Soviet foreign policy = 1.69 + .26 (idealization of American foreign policy). $R^2 = .05,\ F(1,212) = 10.9,\ p(t)$ and $p(F) \leqslant .002,\ SE = 1.49,\ R^2 = .05.$

13. A competing hypothesis—that response checking style on semantic differential items could produce some of the results in this chapter—underlines the importance of the British image comparison (which showed no significant effects) and the (corroborating) concrete attributions made specifically about the Middle East in this item with a different response format.

14. 97.1% of the 102 FSOs and OMB respondents who scored low on neuroticism ($\leqslant 3$) believed the traditional version compared with 83.0% of the 94 who scored high ($\leqslant 3$) on neuroticism. $N = 196,\ \chi^2 = 9.5,\ p(\chi^2) < .003.\ \chi^2$ with Yates correction. Only one military officer was a revisionist, too small a number for a statistical test.

15. A separate analysis showed that, at State and OMB only, those with more neurotic symptoms were more *opposed* to a military confrontation with the Soviet Union in the Caribbean scenario. Opposition went from 26.7% of the 101 with low neuroticism scores ($\leqslant 3$) to 41.9% of the 74 with scores above 3.0. $p(\chi^2) < .06,\ N = 175,\ \chi^2$ with Yates correction = 3.77.

16. Assuming, again, that the equations are properly specified.

17. A one-stage process, such as some earlier psychoanalytic writers seem to have employed, is an index of psychosis since reality cues play no part in establishing appropriateness in such a theory. The two-stage theory sketched here maintains that projection is invoked as an aid to understanding reality, not a process primarily of looking for an excuse to have an enemy that one needs for his own mental stability.

18. As we shall see later in this chapter their age, particularly at the higher levels, also places them in a cohort whose members believe more strongly the traditional explanation of the origins of the cold war.

19. A variety of theories—gestalt, cognitive consistency, Freudian—could be invoked to explore this internal thematic coherence. See Robert P. Abelson et al. (eds.), *Theories of Cognitive Consistency: A Sourcebook* (Chicago: Rand McNally, 1968); John D. Steinbruner, *The Cybernetic Theory of Decision* (Princeton: Princeton University Press, 1974), ch. 4; Robert Jervis, *Perception and Misperception in International Politics* (Princeton: Princeton University Press, 1976); Dina Zinnes, "The Expression and Perception of Hostility in Prewar Crisis, 1914" in J. David Singer (ed.), *Quantitative International Politics: Insights and Evidence* (New York: Free Press, 1968). See the correlation discussed earlier (chapter 3 of the present work), which identifies this syndrome tendency in interpersonal—and again in international—relations.

20. David Rothberg, in an unpublished study of 251 military officers at the Air War College and Air Command and Staff College, reports high scores for TAT power motivation and moderately high correlation between these scores (.55, $p < .001$)

and the fear of having power used against them by others. See David Rothberg, *Insecurity and Success in American Life* (Cambridge, Mass. MIT, doctoral thesis in process); see also David Winter, *The Power Motive* (New York: Free Press, 1973), p. 84 et passim.

21. Robert A. Levine and Donald T. Campbell, *Ethnocentrism: Theories of Conflict, Ethnic Attitudes, and Group Behavior* (New York: Wiley, 1972), pp. 150–155; Philip E. Slater, *Footholds* (New York: Dutton, 1977), chs. 9, 10, and apps. A, B; William Eckhardt, "Anthropological Correlates of Primitive Militarism," *Peace Research,* 5:2 (February, 1973), pp. 5–10; Elbert W. Russell, "Factors of Human Aggression: A Cross-Cultural Factor Analysis of Characteristics Related to Warfare and Crime," *Behavior Science Notes,* 7:4 (1972), pp. 275–312. A recent review of nine major cross-cultural studies of war is David Levinson, "What Have We Learned From Cross-Cultural Surveys?" *American Behavioral Scientist,* 20:5 (May–June, 1977), pp. 757–792. See also the following theoretical pieces on male narcissism: Lloyd Etheredge, "Hardball Politics: A Model" (Unpublished paper presented to the Northeast Political Science Association meeting, 1976); Bruce Mazlish, *The Revolutionary Ascetic* (New York: Basic, 1976); Lucian Pye, *Mao Tse Tung: The Man in the Leader* (New York: Basic Books, 1976); Hudson W. Meadwell, "Male Narcissism and American Foreign Policy" (unpublished manuscript, Duke University, n.d.), Winter (n. 20).

22. Nathan Leites, *A Study of Bolshevism* (Glencoe, Ill.: Free Press, 1954). Leites' theory is different from those of current writers, but the syndrome is similar.

23. Eleanor Maccoby and Carol Jacklin, *The Psychology of Sex Differences* (Stanford: Stanford University Press, 1974); see also the emerging evidence linking the level of the male sex hormone testosterone with aggressiveness, in Joel Ehrenkranz, et al., "Plasma Testosterone: Correlation with Aggressive Behavior and Social Dominance in Man," *Psychosomatic Medicine,* 36:6 (November–December, 1974), pp. 469–475.

24. Another interpretation might also account for linkages between some personality characteristics and the perception of the Soviet Union. The most widely used psychoanalytic version of ethnocentrism conceives the superego and the ego as allied to combat repressed id impulses which an individual has projected into his image of an outgroup. But Bruno Bettelheim and Morris Janowitz have suggested an alternative formulation of *superego* projection which might operate with respect to certain groups. By this formulation it is the id and the ego which ally to resist projected aspects of a harsh and tyrannical superego. In this account the threats to his happiness, freedom, and self-expression which a man may feel are embodied in Soviet foreign policy are, in part, transformed caricatures of the criticisms and demands he would be inclined to make of himself in other areas of his personal life. *If* one considers the image of the ideal self to be what Bettelheim and Janowitz mean by "superego," and *if* what I have called "desires" for activity and power are reconceptualized as superego "demands" on the self, then the findings of this study are evidence for superego projection in forming the image of Soviet foreign policy and the tendency to employ force would be, in part, a playing-out in the global arena

of a man's internal divisions. See Bruno Bettelheim and Morris Janowitz, *Dynamics of Prejudice* (New York: Harper, 1950), p. 43. See also Ray Schafer, *Psychoanalytic Interpretation in Rorshach Testing: Theory and Application* (New York: Grune and Stratton, 1954), p. 279.

25. Richard Sennett and Jonathan Cobb, *The Hidden Injuries of Class* (New York: Knopf, 1972).

26. Kenneth W. Terhune, "Motives, Situation, and Interpersonal Conflict Within Prisoner's Dilemma, *Journal of Personality and Social Psychology,* 8 (1968) monograph 3, part 2.

27. Perceived Soviet responsibility (0 to 10 with 10 being highly traditional) = 5.57 + .06 (Age) + .02(age, NWC slope shift). $p(t)$ respectively $< 5 \times 10^{-4}$ and $< .01$. $F(2,220) = 12.5, p(F) < 8 \times 10^{-2}, R^2 = .10$, SE = 2.10.

28. It would be possible to do a "path analysis" in which, for example, orthodox views of cold war origins and domestic conservatism are intervening variables between personality and desired war capability. But I suspect the exercise would, because of different scale reliabilities, claim too much precision. As well it is not clear the extent to which conservatism or traditional cold war views are in effect qualitatively different variables with independent effects or whether they are *composite* variables which enter into the equations as surrogates for multiple components of ambition, competitiveness, fear, etc., which they embody (and whose variances they absorb) to various degrees.

I have also chosen not to use various high technology data aggregation techniques like factor analysis because it seems to me more important to preserve empathy with the complex and subtle processes actually at work.

Chapter 6

1. R. E. Donley and D. G. Winter, "Measuring the Motives of Public Officials at a Distance: An Exploratory Study of American Presidents," *Behavioral Science,* 15 (1970), pp. 227–236. See also David Winter, *The Power Motive* (New York: Free Press, 1973), pp. 212–218.

2. See David McClelland, *Power: The Inner Experience* (New York: Irvington, 1975) for data which suggest this possibility.

3. William Eckhardt, "Ideology and Personality in Social Attitudes," *Peace Research Reviews,* 3:2 (April, 1969), entire; William Eckhardt and T. Lentz, "Factors of War/Peace Attitudes," *Peace Research Reviews,* 1:5 (October, 1967), entire.

4. I am here following Greenstein's methodological lead. However, I have altered his concept of "actor dispensability" to the slightly more constrained concept of "elite actor interchangeability," a modification which seems more useful for focusing upon different levels of analysis. See Fred I. Greenstein, *Personality and Politics: Problems of Evidence, Inference, and Conceptualization* (Chicago: Markham, 1969), ch. 2.

5. Irving L. Janis, *Victims of Groupthink* (Boston: Houghton Mifflin, 1972). Since shared personality traits can produce policy agreement—and since I have ignored the cases of policy agreement—this research design may underestimate the total impact of elite personality traits.

6. It is conceivable that, with more cases, a less simple and more differentiated approach would be useful. Thus the present personality dimension may predict best to use of force against smaller countries, but relations with autonomously powerful opponents in domestic politics might predict better to relations with the Soviet Union since World War II. For all his bullying tendencies toward subordinates, Lyndon Johnson was more restrained and empathetic in dealing with the Soviet Union.

7. Donley and Winter (n. 1). See the correlation between dominance and ambition in table 3.1. In the State Department study, the failure to selectively measure dominance over subordinates may account for the poor explanatory power of the measure used.

8. The use of trained political scientists can be challenged on the grounds they may bring bias to such tasks. My own feeling is that they bring a useful sensitivity to power. For example, Franklin Roosevelt's chaotic administrative style might be interpreted as reflecting low dominance. The judges, however, saw this as a style consciously designed to heighten presidential dominance. A similar professional sensitivity applies to the Truman coding problem discussed next in the text.

9. Norman A. Graebner (ed.), *An Uncertain Tradition: American Secretaries of State in the Twentieth Century* (New York: McGraw Hill, 1961).

10. Jessup (table 6.2, entry 4), p. 250.

11. Thus among the low dominance men the introverts (Maintainers) should be more likely to use force to maintain the status quo.

12. Schlesinger (table 6.2, entry 22), p. 435.

13. Harold D. Lasswell, *Psychopathology and Politics* (New York: Viking, 1960).

14. To check further whether the dynamics investigated in the historical study corresponded to dynamics that could be confirmed directly by men involved in top level decision-making groups, a summary report of the research was brought to the attention of several participants in foreign policy during the Johnson administration. Former Undersecretary of State George Ball felt strongly that personality explanations were crucial to understanding the Vietnam War, although he felt the better conceptualization was to see decision makers' approaches to policy as a result of past learned and reinforced behavior. He felt that his own belief in the limits of power grew from his post–World War II experience in Europe. He felt that Dean Rusk's approach to Vietnam was essentially a reenactment of Rusk's earlier positive experience in the Korean War (when he had been assistant secretary of state.) Rusk believed, according to Ball, that Vietnam would eventually work out for America and he would explicitly cite the dark days of the Korean War (which had eventually

turned in America's favor). Presidential adviser McGeorge Bundy, Ball felt, was too used to functioning as a college dean, concerned with management of a process rather than substance, and that his successor, Walt Rostow, was similar. Lyndon Johnson, he felt, simply had no elite background and experience to form firm and independent views of his own and tended to act out of awe of his well-educated elite advisers. Secretary of Defense McNamara's past experience with computers led him to concentrate on this technology without sufficient consideration of psychological and political dimensions. See George W. Ball, "A Policy Maker's View: Experience vs. Character," *Psychology Today* (March, 1975), p. 39.

I have no disagreement with George Ball since I think policy outcomes are multiply determined, and the hypothesis that successful personal approaches to past similar problems are carried forward seems promising. (Personality tendencies in these men—since they were all nominally "successful" in terms of American norms— could be seen in the same broad framework.) J. David Barber's notion of the model provided by a "first independent political success" seems relevant here. See J. D. Barber, *The Presidential Character: Predicting Performance in the White House* (Englewood Cliffs: Prentice-Hall, 1972).

Chapter 7

1. See, for example, Eric Klinger, *Structure and Functions of Fantasy* (New York: Wiley Interscience, 1971); David McClelland et al., *The Achievement Motive* (New York: Appleton-Century, 1953) and *Power: The Inner Experience* (New York: Irvington, 1975); David Winter, *The Power Motive* (New York: Free Press, 1973); David McClelland and David Winter, *Motivating Economic Achievement* (New York: Free Press, 1971); J. W. Atkinson (ed.), *Motives in Fantasy, Action, and Society* (Princeton: Van Nostrand, 1958); Bernard Murstein (ed.), *Handbook of Projective Techniques* (New York: Basic Books, 1965); Peter B. Warr (ed.), *Thought and Personality* (Baltimore: Penguin, 1970); Michael Lerner, *Personal Politics* (unpublished Ph.D. dissertation, Yale University, 1971).

2. See, especially, Winter, *The Power Motive* (n. 1).

3. Quoted in Alfred Schuetz, "Choosing Among Projects of Action," *Philosophy and Phenomenological Research,* XII:2 (December, 1951), pp. 161–184, esp. p. 162. See also DeRivera's notion of "shuttling" and linearity, a useful alternative to the rational choice implications that thought is systematic. Joseph DeRivera, *The Psychological Dimension of Foreign Policy* (Columbus: Merrill, 1968), ch. 4, esp. pp. 116–120 and 125–129. Note also that DeRivera's formal model presented at the beginning does not fit perfectly with his examples; his own running commentary is more instructive of how the decision process may operate. Particularly suggestive I think, are his comments on "the existence of an emotional bias . . . that often seems to exist for one of the alternatives" (p. 119), the altering of perceptions and *meanings* of outcomes which occur in the search for a viable alternative (shifts that would not be predicted by a rational choice model), and his observation that "it is interesting to note how often a decision is helped along by asking for the advice of a friend whose advice we know will be in the right direction" (p. 128).

In addition, projective intuitionism probably makes the conduct of foreign policy more stressful because a man is always, in part, conflicting with a projection of part of himself when he is confronting an enemy.

4. I do not try to resolve the problem here of which comes first, the self-expressive perception or the self-expressive policy predisposition, although I suspect it useful to think of perception as more central.

5. Regis Walther, *Orientations and Behavioral Styles of Foreign Service Officers.* Foreign Affairs Personnel Study No. 5 (New York: Carnegie Endowment for International Peace, 1965), p. 43; and R. Rothstein, *Planning, Prediction, and Policymaking in Foreign Affairs* (Boston: Little, Brown, 1972), pp. 137-147 et passim partially support this conclusion by their observations of intuitionism in policy formation.

6. A desire to have or retain *some* orientation which feels right may also be involved; as Robert Lane puts it, "when the giveness of ideas on which one has implicitly guided one's life is questioned there is a loss of orientation which is frightening." Robert E. Lane, *Political Thinking and Consciousness: The Private Life of the Political Mind* (New York: Markham, 1969), p. 315. See also the related concept of "central paranoia" in Jan Pearce and Saul Newton, *The Conditions of Human Growth* (New York: Citadel, 1963).

7. For the ambition-fear syndrome, if Hitler (with his massive fears of French ambition and Jews) was a 10, Kennedy might be at about 5, LBJ at 6, Nixon a 6.5. Such an ambition-mistrust, grandiosity-paranoia syndrome, documented as well with projective test (TAT) research, is not limited to just FSOs and others in this study. See, e.g., the study of the top echelons of the New York Times by Chris Argyris, *Behind the Front Page* (San Francisco: Jossey Bass, 1974).

8. "National security" (personal security) secrecy is one consequence that could be predicted when men do not feel fully confident to face criticism (i.e., when policy is ego-defensive because it is self-expressive and projectively intuitionist). For an early (and not fully psychological) discussion of trends toward closed policy making see H. Bradford Westerfield, "Congress and Closed Politics in National Security Affairs," *Orbis,* X:3 (Fall, 1966), pp. 737-753.

It follows from this study that political decision makers, since they are inevitably trapped within their own minds, and since they ought to entertain skepticism that they truly understand reality and the most effective policies in a given situation, ought to seek out, honor, and more highly value their critics. A tough, clear-thinking critic is the most effective resource available for developing clarity about assumptions and thought processes. See Alexander L. George, "The Case for Multiple Advocacy in Making Foreign Policy," *American Political Science Review* 67:3 (September, 1972), pp. 751-785.

9. I have not emphasized the Vietnam War problem, and I do *not* suggest that personal predispositions were the only reasons for this conflict, although they may have

been decisive on both sides. For a recent study confirming the impact of President Johnson's personality on war policy see Doris Kearns, *Lyndon Johnson and the American Dream* (New York: Harper and Row, 1976).

10. Harold D. Lasswell, *Psychopathology and Politics,* (New York: Viking, 1960), paperback edition, and *World Politics and Personal Insecurity* (New York: Free Press, 1965), paperback edition.

11. See, for example, the evidence in chapter 3 of the present work that self images are close to idealized self images.

Appendix A

1. In fact questionnaires were also sent to 40 additional civilian students at the National War College. Those FSOs at the National War College and additional FSOs contacted at the Foreign Service Institute through the good offices of John Hurley, Jr., and Don Ellson provided 17 additional FSO responses in addition to the 126 from the random sample. Intergroup comparisons in chapter 3 are based on the random sample, while regression results employ the expanded data base.

2. Foreign Service Officers and military officers who returned the questionnaire only after receiving the follow-up letter were compared with those who responded relatively promptly. I hypothesized that late returns might come from those who were more reluctant to participate and thus the analysis might give a clue to the characteristics of men who were very reluctant and did not return the questionnaire at all. However no significant pattern of differences emerged beyond the level that might be expected from chance.

3. My guess is that about one-half of the subject loss at State and NWC can be attributed to this fact, to time pressures, and to general skepticism about, and lack of interest in, social science research. Personal interviews conducted by Mennis at the Department of State obtained an 80% response rate, similar to that obtained with personal contacts at OMB. Previous mail solicitations of FSOs have produced response rates ranging from 43% to 72%. But many things varied in these studies: world-wide versus Washington samples, subject matter, length of questionnaire, status of the researcher, and there is an insufficient base of experience to infer the reasons for subject loss.

4. These impressions were not based on systematic inquiry. Procedures to guarantee anonymity also precluded my identification of individuals who did not respond.

5. Jeanne Knutson, *The Human Basis of the Polity: A Psychological Study of Political Men* (Chicago: Aldine Atherton, 1972).

6. John Bartlow Martin, *Overtaken by Events* (Garden City: Doubleday, 1966).

7. However it is almost certainly true that the general characteristics of the period affect the responses and make the means different from what might be obtained at another time (e.g., during the height of the cold war) or for another country.

8. Standard additional precautions were also employed: each of the three adjective scales representing five dimensions selected from previous research had one scale reverse-ordered at random.

9. In addition the Leary checklist is counter balanced for social desireability and the Eysenck does not correlate with measures of faking to give a socially approved response. Since social-desireability effects probably operate in the real world, it probably gives the policy choice items more predictive validity not to control for such effects (even if that were possible).

10. David Garnham (personal communication) also reports a readiness of FSOs to "talk back" and object to questions and response alternatives with which they are uncomfortable.

11. See the thesis version, pp. 313–315, for the factor loadings.

12. Ibid.

13. For a general review of problems and methods pertinent to determining factorial structures see Philip Levy, "Concept Scale Interaction in Semantic Differential Research: Solutions in Search of a Problem," *British Journal of Psychology,* 63:2 (1972), pp. 235–236; Murray Miron, "Universal Semantic Differential Shell Game," *Journal of Personality and Social Psychology,* 24:3 (1972), pp. 313–320; John Bynner and David Romney, "A Method for Overcoming the Problem of Concept-Scale Interaction in Semantic Differential Research," *British Journal of Psychology,* 63:2 (1972), pp. 229–234; David Klemmack and John Ballweg, "Concept-Scale Interaction with the Semantic Differential Technique," *Journal of Psychology,* 84 (1973), pp. 345–352. On dimensional structures found for different individuals or groups in international relations research see, for example, J. Robinson and R. Hefner, "Perceptual Maps of the World," *Public Opinion Quarterly,* 32 (Summer, 1968), pp. 273–280; M. Wish et al., Differences in Conceptual Structures of Nations: An Exploratory Study," *Journal of Personality and Social Psychology,* 16 (1970), pp. 361–373; Peter Warr et al., "The Structure of Political Judgement," *British Journal of Social and Clinical Psychology,* 8 (1969), pp. 32–43.

14. However this precaution may have been unnecessary; further analysis using standard Likert summation across scales showed the same pattern of correlations. All results reported for Likert scales in the text were also significant when intensity weighting was dropped.

15. The entire model was also run to determine whether the added controls would significantly alter the results. It should be noted that, when an intercept shift term and an intercept shift–independent variable interaction term for the same group are present in the equation simultaneously the two terms have a high degree of multicollinearity and, while the computed coefficients are best estimates, they would probably be subject to considerable variation given the addition or deletion of a few cases.

16. It is also possible that mood at the time of administration (especially annoyance at the questionnaire) might affect response. A separate check on (self-report) mood showed 12% of military officers, 14% of FSOs, and 8% at OMB were tired. An "annoyance" cluster showed 10% NWC, 4% FSO, and 0% OMB were annoyed by the questionnaire itself in some way. Later analysis showed that there were no significant systematic effects associated with these different moods.

17. I suggest that any remaining imperfections in the two studies *increase* the confidence it is appropriate to place in the results: "once a proposition has been confirmed by two or more independent measurement processes, the uncertainty of its interpretation is greatly reduced. The most persuasive evidence comes through a triangulation of measurement processes. If a proposition can survive the onslaught of a series of imperfect measures, with all their irrelevant error, confidence should be placed in it." Eugene Webb, et al., *Unobtrusive Measures: Nonreactive Research in the Social Sciences* (Chicago: Rand McNally, 1966), p. 3.

18. For a discussion of these issues see Allen W. Wicker, "Attitudes versus Actions: The Relationship of Verbal and Overt Behavioral Responses to Attitude Objects," *Journal of Social Issues,* 25:4 (1969), pp. 41–78; Robert P. Abelson, "Are Attitudes Necessary?" in Bert T. King and Elliott McGinnies (eds.), *Attitudes, Conflict, and Social Change* (New York: Academic Press, 1972), pp. 19–32; M. Brewster Smith, "Political Attitudes" in Jeanne Knutson (ed.), *Handbook of Political Psychology* (San Francisco: Jossey Bass, 1973), pp. 57–82, esp. p. 77; Icek Ajzen and Martin Fishbein, "Attitude-Behavior Relations: A Theoretical Analysis and Review of Empirical Research," *Psychological Bulletin,* 84:5 (September, 1977), pp. 888–918. My own position is close to the Abelson-Smith views.

19. From McClosky Jingoist Isolation scale. See Herbert McClosky, "Personality and Attitude Correlates of Foreign Policy Orientation," in James Rosenau (ed.), *Domestic Sources of Foreign Policy* (New York: Free Press, 1967), p. 103.

   The use of "sloganistic" or emotionally-expressive attitude items in most personality-attitude research generates a potentially serious validity problem when extrapolating to elites. If *all* a man can record is his emotionally-expressive response, then the results may *overstate* the extent of emotional factors in the involvement (which will include cognitive processing) evidenced by sophisticated men in actual situations.

20. One indication of this possibility is that the interpersonal dominance scale of the Leary Interpersonal Checklist (ICL) did not predict to the use of force, while dominance over subordinates was a strong predictor in the historical study. Of course the Leary ICL is not as good a measure as the direct observations used in the historical study, but the anomaly suggests the possibility that dominating tendencies may be more strongly generalized in foreign policy when the man is in the driver's seat rather than on the sidelines.

21. See, for example, the general discussion in J. Johnston, *Econometric Methods,* second edition (New York: McGraw Hill, 1972), pp. 281–291. Discussions of this

problem with respect to psychological tests may be found in Karl Schuessler, *Analyzing Social Data: A Statistical Orientation* (Boston: Houghton Mifflin, 1971), ch. 8, and Frederic Lord and Melvin Novick, *Statistical Theories of Mental Test Scores* (Reading: Addison-Wesley, 1968), pp. 69–74 and 137–138. I should emphasize that the direction of, and size of, adjustments are straightforward only in the bivariate case.

Bibliography

Abelson, R., *et al.* (eds), *Theories of Cognitive Consistency: A Sourcebook* (Chicago: Rand McNally, 1968).

Abrahamsson, Bengt, *Military Professionalization and Political Power* (Beverly Hills: Sage, 1972).

Adams, Sherman, *First-Hand Report* (New York: Harper, 1961).

Ajzen, Icek and Fishbein, Martin, "Attitude-Behavior Relations: A Theoretical Analysis and Review of Empirical Research," *Psychological Bulletin* 84:5 (September, 1977), pp. 888–918.

Allison, Graham T., *Essence of Decision: Explaining the Cuban Missile Crisis* (Boston: Little, Brown, 1971).

Argyris, Chris, *Behind the Front Page* (San Francisco: Jossey Bass, 1974).

Argyris, Chris, *Some Causes of Organizational Ineffectiveness Within the Department of State,* Occasional Paper No. 2 of the Center for International Systems Research (Washington: State Department, 1967).

Atkinson, J. W., (ed.), *Motives in Fantasy, Action, and Society* (Princeton: Van Nostrand, 1958).

Atkinson, Tom, *A Propositional Inventory of Empirical Work Involving Foreign Affairs and National Security Attitudes, 1960-1966* (Oak Ridge: Oak Ridge National Laboratory, 1967).

Bailey, Thomas A., *A Diplomatic History of the American People,* eighth edition (New York: Appleton-Century-Crofts, 1968).

Ball, George W., "A Policy Maker's View: Experience vs. Character," *Psychology Today* (March, 1975), p. 39.

Barber, James D., *The Lawmakers* (New Haven: Yale University Press, 1965).

Barber, James D., *Power in Committees: An Experiment in the Governmental Process* (Chicago: Rand McNally, 1966).

Barber, James D., *The Presidential Character* (Englewood Cliffs: Prentice-Hall, 1972).

Beale, Howard K., *Theodore Roosevelt and the Rise of America to World Power* (Baltimore: Johns Hopkins Press, 1956).

Bettelheim, Bruno and Janowitz, Morris, *Dynamics of Prejudice* (New York: Harper, 1950).

Bynner, John and Romney, David, "A Method for Overcoming the Problem of Concept-Scale Interaction in Semantic Differential Research," *British Journal of Psychology,* 63:2 (1972), pp. 229–234.

Campbell, Donald T., "Reforms as Experiments" in James Caporaso and Leslie Roos, Jr. (eds). *Quasi-Experimental Approaches* (Evanston: Northwestern University Press, 1973).

Challener, Richard, "William Jennings Bryan" in Norman A. Graebner (ed.), *An Uncertain Tradition: American Secretaries of State in the Twentieth Century* (New York: McGraw Hill, 1961), pp. 79-100.

Chesterton, G. K., "The Mistake of the Machine," in his *The Wisdom of Father Brown* (Middlesex: Penguin, 1970), pp. 76-91.

Christiansen, Bjorn, *Attitudes Towards Foreign Affairs as a Function of Personality* (Oslo: Oslo University Press, 1959).

Clinch, Nancy, *The Kennedy Neurosis* (New York: Grosset and Dunlop, 1973).

Curti, Merle, "Bryan and World Peace," *Smith College Studies in History,* 16: 3-4 (April–July, 1931), entire.

D'Amato, Anthony A., "Psychological Constructs in Foreign Policy Prediction," *Journal of Conflict Resolution,* II (1967), pp. 294-311.

Davies, James C., "Aggression, Violence, Revolution, and War" in Jeanne Knutson (ed.), *Handbook of Political Psychology* (San Francisco: Jossey-Bass, 1973), pp. 234-260.

DeRivera, Joseph, *The Psychological Dimension of Foreign Policy* (Columbus: Merrill, 1968).

Deutsch, Karl W., *The Analysis of International Relations* (Englewood Cliffs: Prentice-Hall, 1968).

Deutsch, Karl W., and Senghaas, Dieter, "The Steps to War: A Survey of System Levels, Decision Stages, and Research Results" in Patrick J. McGowan (ed.), *Sage International Yearbook of Foreign Policy Studies,* vol. 1 (Beverly Hills: Sage, 1973).

Donley, R. E., and Winter, D. G., "Measuring the Motives of Public Officials at a Distance: An Exploratory Study of American Presidents," *Behavioral Science,* 15 (1970) pp. 227-236.

Dougherty, James E., and Pfaltzgraff, Robert, *Contending Theories of International Relations* (Philadelphia: Lippincott, 1971).

Dulles, Foster Rhea, "John Hay" in Norman A. Graebner (ed.), *An Uncertain Tradition: American Secretaries of State in the Twentieth Century* (New York: McGraw Hill, 1961). pp. 22-39.

Eckhardt, William, "Ideology and Personality in Social Attitudes," *Peace Research Reviews,* III: 2 (April, 1969) entire.

Eckhardt, William, "The Military Industrial Personality," *Journal of Contemporary Revolutions,* 3: 4 (1971), pp. 74-87.

Eckhardt, William, and Alcock, N., "Ideology and Personality in War/Peace Attitudes," *Journal of Social Psychology,* 81 (1970), pp. 105-116.

Eckhardt, William and Lentz, Theo., "Factors of War/Peace Attitudes," *Peace Research Reviews,* I: 5 (October, 1967), entire.

Ehrenkranz, Joel, et al., "Plasma Testosterone: Correlation with Aggressive Behavior and Social Dominance in Man," *Psychosomatic Medicine,* 36:6 (November–December, 1974), pp. 469-475.

Erikson, Erik, *Gandhi's Truth* (New York: Norton, 1969).

Erikson, Erik, *Young Man Luther* (New York: Norton, 1958).

Etheredge, Lloyd, *The Case of the Unreturned Cafeteria Trays* (Washington: American Political Science Association, 1976).

Etheredge, Lloyd, "Hardball Politics: A Model" (Forthcoming).

Etheredge, Lloyd, "Hypnosis and Order" in John Sweeney (ed.), *Politics and Society* (forthcoming).

Etheredge, Lloyd, *Political Psychology and Qualitative Metaphysics* (unpublished manuscript).

Etheredge, Lloyd, *A World of Men: The Private Sources of American Foreign Policy* (doctoral thesis, Yale University, 1974; University Microfilms).

Etzioni, Amitai, "Social Psychological Aspects of International Relations" in G. Lindzey and E. Aronson (eds.), *The Handbook of Social Psychology,* second edition (Reading, Mass.: Addison-Wesley, 1969), vol. 5, pp. 538-601.

Eysenck, H. H., "A Short Questionnaire for the Measurement of Two Dimensions of Personality," *Journal of Applied Psychology,* 42:1 (1958), pp. 14-17.

Fitzgerald, Frances, *Fire in the Lake: The Vietnamese and the Americans in Vietnam* (New York: Random House, 1972).

Garnham, David C., "Attitude and Personality Patterns of United States Foreign Service Officers," *American Journal of Political Science,* 18:3 (1974), pp. 31-39.

Garnham, David, *Attitude and Personality Patterns of Foreign Service Officers and the Conduct of American Foreign Affairs* (unpublished doctoral dissertation, University of Minnesota, 1971).

Garnham, David, "State Department Rigidity: Testing a Psychological Hypothesis," *International Studies Quarterly,* 18:1 (1974), pp. 31-39.

George Alexander, "The Case for Multiple Advocacy in Making Foreign Policy," *American Political Science Review,* 67:3 (September, 1972), pp. 751-785.

George, Alexander, "The Operational Code: A Neglected Approach to the Study of Political Leaders and Decision-Making," *International Studies Quarterly,* 13 (1969), pp. 109-222.

George, Alexander and George, Juliette, *Woodrow Wilson and Colonel House* (New York: Dover, 1964).

Gergen, Kenneth, "Social Psychology as History," *Journal of Personality and Social Psychology,* 26:2 (1973), pp. 309-320.

Geyelin, Philip, *Lyndon B. Johnson and the World* (New York: Praeger, 1966).

Glad, Betty, *Charles Evans Hughes and the Illusions of Innocence* (Urbana: University of Illinois Press, 1966).

Goldmann, Kjell, *International Norms and War Between States* (Stockholm: Laromedelsforlagen, 1971).

Graebner, Norman A. (ed.), *An Uncertain Tradition: American Secretaries of State in the Twentieth Century* (New York: McGraw Hill, 1961).

Greenstein, Fred I., *Personality and Politics: Problems of Evidence, Inference, and Conceptualization* (Chicago: Markham, 1969).

Halberstam, David, *The Best and the Brightest* (New York: Random House, 1972).

Halperin, Morton, et al., *Bureaucratic Politics and Foreign Policy* (Washington, DC: Brookings Institution, 1974).

Hamilton, David L., "The Comparative Study of Five Methods of Assessing Self-Esteem, Dominance, and Dogmatism," *Educational and Psychological Measurement,* 31 (Summer, 1971), pp. 441–452.

Hanushek, Eric A. and Jackson, John E., *Statistical Methods for Social Scientists* (New York: Academic Press, 1977).

Harbough, W. H., *The Life and Times of Theodore Roosevelt,* rev. ed. (New York: Collier, 1963).

Harbough, W. H., *Power and Responsibility: The Life and Times of Theodore Roosevelt* (New York: Farrar, Strauss, and Cudahy, 1961).

Harr, John Ensor, *The Professional Diplomat* (Princeton: Princeton University Press, 1969).

Hermann, Charles F. (ed.), *International Crisis: Insights from Behavioral Science* (New York: Free Press, 1972).

Hermann, Margaret, "Effect of Personal Characteristics of Leaders on Foreign Policy" in M. A. East et al. (eds.), *Why Nations Act* (Beverly Hills: Sage, 1977).

Hermann, Margaret, "How Leaders Process Information and the Effect on Foreign Policy: An Exploratory Study" in James N. Rosenau (ed.), *Comparing Foreign Policies: Theories, Findings, and Methods* (Beverly Hills: Sage, 1974).

Hilsman, Roger, *To Move a Nation* (New York: Doubleday, 1967).

Holsti, Ole, "Cognitive Dynamics and Images of the Enemy: Dulles and Russia" in David Finlay et al., *Enemies in Politics* (Chicago: Rand McNally, 1967), pp. 25–96.

Holsti, Ole, "Foreign Policy Formation Viewed Cognitively" in Robert M. Axelrod (ed.), *Structure of Decision: The Cognitive Maps of Political Elites* (Princeton: Princeton University Press, 1976), pp. 18–54.

Holsti, Ole, "The 'Operational Code' Approach to the Study of Political Leaders: John Foster Dulles' Philosophical and Instrumental Beliefs," *Canadian Journal of Political Science,* III:1 (March, 1970), pp. 123–157.

Holsti, Ole, and George, Alexander L., "Adaptation to Stress in Political Decision Making: the Individual, Small Group and Organizational Contexts," in G. V. Coelho et al. (eds.), *Coping and Adaptation* (New York: Basic Books, 1974).

Hoover, Herbert, *The Memoirs of Herbert Hoover: The Cabinet and the Presidency, 1920–1933* (New York: Macmillan, 1952).

Hughes, Emmet J., *The Ordeal of Power: A Political Memoir of the Eisenhower Years* (New York: Atheneum, 1963).

Janis, Irving, and Mann, Leon, *Decision Making: A Psychological Analysis of Conflict, Choice and Commitment* (New York: Free Press, 1977).

Janis, Irving, *Victims of Groupthink: A Psychological Study of Foreign-Policy Decisions and Fiascoes* (Boston: Houghton Mifflin, 1972).

Jaszi, Oscar, The *Dissolution of the Hapsburg Monarchy* (Chicago: University of Chicago Press, 1929), paperback edition, 1961.

Jensen, Lloyd, "Foreign Policy Calculation" in Michael Haas (ed.), *International Systems: A Behavioral Approach* (New York: Chandler, 1974), pp. 77–97.

Jervis, Robert, *Perception and Misperception in International Relations* (Princeton: Princeton University Press, 1976).

Jessup, Philip, *Elihu Root,* 2 vols. (New York: Dodd, Mead, 1938), Archon Books edition, 1964.

Johnston, J., *Econometric Methods,* second edition (New York: McGraw-Hill, 1972).

Kail, F. M., *What Washington Said: Administration Rhetoric and the Vietnam War* (New York: Harper and Row, 1973).

Kaplan, Morton, *On Historical and Political Knowing* (Chicago: University of Chicago Press, 1971).

Kearns, Doris, *Lyndon Johnson and the American Dream* (New York: Harper and Row, 1976).

Kelman, Herbert, "The Role of the Individual in International Relations: Some Conceptual and Methodological Considerations," *Journal of International Affairs,* 24:1 (1970), pp. 1–17.

Kelman, Herbert and Bloom, Alfred, "Assumptive Frameworks in International Politics" In Jeanne Knutson (ed.), *Handbook of Political Psychology* (San Francisco: Jossey-Bass, 1973), pp. 261–295.

Kennan, George F., "American Involvement" in Marcus G. Raskin and Bernard B. Fall (eds.), *The Viet-Nam Reader* (New York: Vintage, 1967), revised edition, pp. 15–31.

Kennan, George F., *Memoirs, 1925-1950* (New York: Bantam Books, 1967).

Kennan, George F., *Memoirs, 1950-1963* (Boston: Little, Brown, 1972).

Kennan, George F., "The Statement and Testimony of the Honorable George F. Kennan," in J. William Fulbright (ed.), *The Vietnam Hearings* (New York: Random House, 1966), pp. 107-166.

Kirkpatrick, Samuel A., "Psychological Views of Decision-Making" in Cornelius P. Cotter (ed.), *Political Science Annual: Individual Decision Making* (Indianapolis: Bobbs-Merrill, 1975).

Kissinger, Henry A., "Domestic Structure and Foreign Policy," *Daedalus,* XCV (Spring, 1966), pp. 503-529.

Kite, W. R., *Attributions of Causality as a Function of the Use of Reward and Punishment* (unpublished doctoral dissertation, Stanford University, 1964).

Klemmack, David and Ballweg, John, "Concept-Scale Interaction with the Semantic Differential Technique," *Journal of Psychology,* 84 (1973), pp. 345-352.

Klinger, Eric, *Structure and Functions of Fantasy* (New York: Wiley Interscience, 1971).

Knorr, Klaus, and Verba, Sidney (eds.), *The International System: Theoretical Essays* (Princeton: Princeton University Press, 1961).

Knutson, Jeanne, *The Human Basis of the Polity: A Psychological Study of Political Men* (Chicago: Aldine-Atherton, 1972).

Knutson, Jeanne, "Personality in the Study of Politics" in Jeanne Knutson (ed.), *Handbook of Political Psychology* (San Francisco: Jossey-Bass, 1973), pp. 28-56.

LaFeber, Walter, *The New Empire: An Interpretation of American Expansion 1860-1898* (Ithaca: Cornell University Press, 1963).

LaForge, Rolfe, et al., "The Interpersonal Dimension of Personality: II. An Objective Study of Repression," *Journal of Personality,* 23:1 (September, 1954), pp. 129-153.

Lane, Robert E., *Political Ideology: Why the American Common Man Believes What He Does* (Glencoe: Free Press, 1962).

Lane, Robert E., *Political Thinking and Consciousness: The Private Life of the Political Mind* (New York: Markham, 1969).

Langer, Walter C., *The Mind of Adolph Hitler* (New York: Basic Books, 1972).

Lasswell, Harold D., *Power and Personality* (New York: Norton, 1948).

Lasswell, Harold D., *Psychopathology and Politics* (Chicago: University of Chicago Press, 1930).

Lasswell, Harold D., *World Politics and Personal Insecurity* (New York: Free Press, 1965).

Lefberg, Irving, *Analyzing Judicial Change: the Uses of Systematic Biography* (unpublished doctoral thesis in progress, M.I.T.).

Leites, Nathan A., *A Study of Bolshevism* (Glencoe, Ill.: Free Press, 1954).

Lerche, Charles O., Jr., "The Professional Officer and Foreign Policy," *Strategic Subjects Handbook* (Fort Leavenworth: US Army Command and General Staff College, 1967), R 1800-1, p. Li–5f.

Lerner, Michael, *Personal Politics* (unpublished doctoral dissertation, Yale University, 1971).

LeVine, Robert A. and Campbell, Donald T., *Ethnocentrism: Theories of Conflict, Ethnic Attitudes, and Group Behavoir* (New York: Wiley, 1972).

Levinson, David, "What Have We Learned from Cross-Cultural Surveys?" *American Behavioral Scientist* 20:5 (May–June, 1977), pp. 757–792.

Levy, Philip, "Concept-Scale Interaction in Semantic Differential Research: Solutions in Search of a Problem," *British Journal of Psychology,* 63:2 (1972), pp. 235–236.

Lord, Ferderic and Novick, Melvin, *Statistical Theories of Mental Test Scores* (Reading, Mass.: Addison-Wesley, 1968).

Maccoby, Eleanor, and Jacklin, Carol, *The Psychology of Sex Differences* (Stanford: Stanford University Press, 1974).

Martin, John Bartlow, *Overtaken By Events* (Garden City: Doubleday, 1966).

Marton, Endre, "Kennan Decries Talk of Détente: He Sees No Atmosphere of East-West Cooperation," The New York Times, September 22, 1968, p. 3.

Mazlish, Bruce, *In Search of Nixon* (New York: Basic Books, 1972).

Mazlish, Bruce, *Kissinger: the European Mind in American Politics* (New York: Basic Books, 1976).

Mazlish, Bruce, *The Revolutionary Ascetic* (New York: Basic Books, 1976).

McClelland, David, et al., *The Achievement Motive* (New York: Appleton-Century, 1953).

McClelland, David, *Power: The Inner Experience* (New York: Irvington, 1975).

McClelland, David and Winter, David, *Motivating Economic Achievement* (New York: Free Press, 1971).

McClosky, Herbert, "Personality and Attitude Correlates of Foreign Policy Orientation," in James N. Rosenau (ed.), *Domestic Sources of Foreign Policy* (New York: Free Press, 1967), pp. 51–109.

Meadwell, Hudson W., "Male Narcissism and American Foreign Policy" (unpublished manuscript, Duke University, n.d.).

Mennis, Bernard, *American Foreign Policy Officials: Who They Are and What They Believe Regarding International Politics* (Columbus: Ohio State University Press, 1971).

Meyer, K. E., and Szulc, T., *The Cuban Invasion* (New York: Praeger, 1962).

Miron, Murray, "Universal Semantic Differential Shell Game," *Journal of Personality and Social Psychology,* 24:3 (1972), pp. 313–320.

Morgenthau, Hans, "John Foster Dulles" in Norman A. Graebner (ed.), *An Uncertain Tradition: American Secretaries of State in the Twentieth Century* (New York: McGraw-Hill, 1961), pp. 289–308.

Morison, Elting, *Turmoil and Tradition: A Study of the Life and Times of Henry L. Stimson* (Boston: Houghton Mifflin, 1960).

Muller, H., *Adlai Stevenson: A Study of Values* (New York: Harper and Row, 1967).

Murray, Robert K., *The Harding Era* (Minneapolis: University of Minneapolis Press, 1969).

Murstein, Bernard (ed.), *Handbook of Projective Techniques* (New York: Basic Books, 1965).

Nelson, Stephen, "Nature/Nuture Revisited I: A Review of the Biological Bases of Conflict," *Journal of Conflict Resolution,* 18 (1974), pp. 285–335.

Noble, G. Bernard, *Christian Herter* (New York: Cooper Square, 1970), vol. 18 of S. F. Bemis and R. H. Ferrell (eds.), *The American Secretaries of State and Their Diplomacy.*

Osgood, Charles, et al., *The Measurement of Meaning* (Urbana: University of Illinois Press, 1957).

Pearce, Jan, and Newton, Saul, *The Conditions of Human Growth* (New York: Citadel, 1963).

Pearson, Lester B., *Partners in Development: Report of the Commission on International Development* (New York: Praeger, 1969).

Pye, Lucian, *Mao Tse Tung: The Man in the Leader* (New York: Basic Books, 1976).

Randle, Robert, *Geneva 1954* (Princeton: Princeton University Press, 1969).

Raser, John, "Personal Characteristics of Political Decision-Makers: A Literature Review," *Papers of the Peace Research Society (International),* 5 (1966), pp. 16–181.

Robinson, John P., et al., *Measures of Political Attitudes* (Ann Arbor: Survey Research Center, 1968).

Robinson, J. and Hefner, R., "Perceptual Maps of the World," *Public Opinion Quarterly,* 32 (Summer, 1968), pp. 273–280.

Robinson, John and Shaver, Phillip, *Measures of Social Psychological Attitudes* (Ann Arbor: Survey Research Center, 1969).

Rogow, Arnold, *James Forrestal: A Study of Personality, Politics, and Policy* (New York: Macmillan, 1963).

Rothberg, David, *Insecurity and Success in American Life* (doctoral thesis in progress. M.I.T.).

Rothstein, Robert L., *Planning, Prediction, and Policymaking in Foreign Affairs* (Boston: Little, Brown, 1972).

Russell, Elbert W., "Factors of Human Aggression: A Cross-Cultural Analysis of Characteristics Related to Warfare and Crime," *Behavior Science Notes,* 7:4 (1972), pp. 275–312.

Russett, Bruce M., "Demography, Salience, and Internationalist Behavior," *Public Opinion Quarterly,* 24 (1960), pp. 658–664.

Schafer, Roy, *Psychoanalytic Interpretation in Rorschach Testing: Theory and Application* (New York: Grune and Stratton, 1954).

Schlenker, Barry, and Tedeschi, James, "Interpersonal Attraction and the Exercise of Coercive and Reward Power," *Human Relations,* 25:5 (1973).

Schlesinger, Arthur M., Jr., *A Thousand Days: John F. Kennedy in the White House* (Boston: Houghton Mifflin, 1965).

Schubert, Glendon, *Quantitative Analysis of Judicial Behavior* (Glencoe: Free Press, 1959).

Schuessler, Karl, *Analyzing Social Data: A Statistical Orientation* (Boston: Houghton Mifflin, 1971).

Schuetz, Alfred, "Choosing Among Projects of Action," *Philosophy and Phenomenological Research,* XII:2 (December, 1951), pp. 161–184.

Scott, James Brown, "Robert Bacon" in Samuel F. Bemis (ed.), *The American Secretaries of State and Their Diplomacy* (New York: Cooper Square, 1963), vol. 9, pp. 283–299.

Scott, James Brown, *Robert Bacon: Life and Letters* (New York: Doubleday Page, 1923).

Scott, William, "International Ideology and Interpersonal Ideology," *Public Opinion Quarterly,* 24 (1960), pp. 419–435.

Semmel, Andrew, "Some Correlates of Foreign Policy Attitudes Among Foreign Service Officers" (unpublished doctoral thesis, University of Michigan, 1972).

Sennett, Richard and Cobb, Jonathan, *The Hidden Injuries of Class* (New York: Vintage, 1972).

Slater, Philip, *Footholds* (New York: Dutton, 1977).

Slater, Philip E., *The Glory of Hera: Greek Mythology and the Greek Family* (Boston: Beacon, 1968).

Smith, Gaddis, "Dean Acheson," in Robert H. Ferrell and Samuel F. Bemis (eds.), *The American Secretaries of State and Their Diplomacy* (New York: Cooper Square, 1972), vol. 16.

Smith, M. Brewster, "A Map for the Analysis of Personality and Politics" reprinted in Fred I. Greenstein and Michael Lerner (eds.), *A Sourcebook for the Analysis of Personality and Politics* (Chicago: Markham, 1971), pp. 34–44.

Smith, M. Brewster, "Political Attitudes" in Jeanne Knutson (ed.), *Handbook of Political Psychology* (San Francisco: Jossey-Bass, 1973), pp. 57–82.

Snider, J., and Osgood, C., (eds.), *Semantic Differential Technique: A Sourcebook* (Chicago: Aldine Press, 1969).

Sniderman, Paul and Citrin, Jack, "Psychological Sources of Political Belief: Self-Esteem and Isolationist Attitudes," *American Political Science Review,* LXV:2 (June, 1971), pp. 401–417.

Sorenson, Theodore, *Kennedy* (New York: Bantam, 1966).

Steinbruner, John D., *The Cybernetic Theory of Decision* (Princeton: Princeton University Press, 1974).

Sumner, William Graham, *Folkways,* (New York: Ginn, 1906).

Terhune, Kenneth W., "The Effects of Personality in Cooperation and Conflict" in Paul Swingle (ed.), *The Structure of Conflict* (New York: Academic Press, 1970), pp. 193–204.

Terhune, Kenneth W., "Motives, Situation, and Interpersonal Conflict within Prisoner's Dilemma," *Journal of Personality and Social Psychology,* 8 (1968), monograph 3, part 2.

Thayer, William, *The Life and Letters of John Hay,* 2 vols. (Boston: Houghton Mifflin, 1915).

Toland, John *Adolph Hitler* (New York: Doubleday, 1976).

Toth, Charles, "Elihu Root" in Norman A. Graebner (ed.), *An Uncertain Tradition: American Secretaries of State in the Twentieth Century* (New York: McGraw Hill, 1969), pp. 40–58.

Tucker, Robert, "The Georges' Wilson Reexamined: an Essay on Psychobiography," *American Political Science Review,* 71:2 (June, 1977), pp. 606–618.

Tucker, Robert, *Stalin as Revolutionary 1879-1929* (New York: Norton, 1974).

Verba, Sidney, "Assumptions of Rationality and Non-Rationality in Models of the International System," in Klaus Knorr and Sidney Verba (eds.), *The International System: Theoretical Essays* (Princeton: Princeton University Press, 1961), pp. 93–117.

Walther, Regis, *Orientations and Behavioral Styles of Foreign Service Officers,* Foreign Affairs Personnel Study No. 5 (New York: Carnegie Endowment for International Peace, 1965).

Waltz, Kenneth, "Theory of International Relations" in Fred I. Greenstein and Nelson Polsby (eds.), *Handbook of Political Science* (Reading: Addison-Wesley, 1975), vol. 8, pp. 1–85.

Warr, Peter B. (ed.), *Thought and Personality* (Baltimore: Penguin, 1970).

Warr, Peter, et al., "The Structure of Political Judgement," *British Journal of Social and Clinical Psychology,* 8 (1969), pp. 32–43.

Webb, Eugene, et al., *Unobtrusive Measures: Nonreactive Research in the Social Sciences* (Chicago: Rand McNally, 1966).

Weintal, Edward, and Bartlett, Charles, *Facing the Brink* (New York: Scribners, 1967).

Westerfield, H. Bradford, "Congress and Closed Politics in National Security Affairs," *Orbis,* X:3 (Fall, 1966), pp. 737–753).

Wheeler, C. L., and Carnes, E. F., "Relations among Self-Concepts, Ideal Self-Concepts, and Stereotypes of Probable and Ideal Vocational Choices," *Journal of Counseling Psychology,* 15 (1968), pp. 530–535.

Wicker, Allen W., "Attitudes versus Actions: the Relationship of Verbal and Overt Behavioral Responses to Attitude Objects," *Journal of Social Issues,* 25:4 (1969), pp. 41–78.

Winter, David, *The Power Motive* (New York: Free Press, 1973), pp. 212–218.

Wish, Myron, et al., "Differences in Conceptual Structures of Nations: An Exploratory Study," *Journal of Personality and Social Psychology,* 16 (1970), pp. 361–373.

Wright, Quincy, *A Study of War* (Chicago: University of Chicago Press, 1964), abridged edition.

Wylie, Ruth C., "The Present Status of Self Theory" in Edgar F. Borgatta and William W. Lambert (eds.), *Handbook of Personality Theory and Research* (Chicago: Rand McNally, 1968), pp. 728–787.

Wylie, Ruth C., *The Self Concept* (Lincoln: University of Nebraska Press, 1961).

Zinnes, Dina, "The Expression and Perception of Hostility in Prewar Crisis, 1914" in J. David Singer (ed.), *Quantitative International Politics: Insights and Evidence* (New York: Free Press, 1968).

Index